D1737465

RICE RECIPES

FROM AROUND THE WORLD

世界の米料理

RICE RECIPES

FROM AROUND THE WORLD

By TOMI EGAMI

Photographs by
YOSHIKATSU SAEKI

KODANSHA INTERNATIONAL LTD.
Tokyo, New York & San Francisco

DISTRIBUTORS:

United States: Harper & Row, Publishers, Inc.
10 East 53rd Street, New York, New York 10022

Canada: Fitzhenry & Whiteside Limited
150 Lesmill Road, Don Mills, Ontario

British Commonwealth (excluding Canada and the Far East):
TABS
51 Weymouth Street, London W1

Europe: Boxerbooks Inc.
Limmatsrasse 111, 8031 Zurich

The Far East: Japan Publications Trading Company
P.O. Box 5030, Tokyo International

Published by Kodansha International Ltd., 2-12-21 Otowa,
Bunkyo-ku, Tokyo 112 and Kodansha International/USA, Ltd.,
10 East 53rd Street, New York, New York 10022 and 44 Mont-
gomery Street, San Francisco, California 94104. Copyright © in
Japan 1966 by Kodansha International Ltd. All rights reserved.
Printed in Japan.

LCC 66-16733
ISBN 0-87011-237-6
JBC 2377-784601-2361

First edition, 1966
First paperback edition, 1974

Table of Contents

SAVORY

Preface

WHY A BOOK of rice recipes? Tomi Egami has been planning this book for many years—partly because, as a Japanese, she sees rice as an important food, partly because she comes from an area where rice is abundant and of excellent quality (she has happy childhood memories of its planting, harvesting and storing and the colorful ceremonies involved), and finally because her travels and experience have convinced her of the worldwide popularity of rice and the universality of its use. This collection of international recipes, representing years of research and experiment, is evidence of the wide appeal rice has, not only for the people of Asia but also for those of the Middle East and the West.

In most Asian countries, as everyone knows, rice has always been the main course, accompanied by a small portion of meat, fish, vegetables or fruit. Tomi Egami recalls her regret during World War II, when rice was strictly rationed in Japan, that she did not know enough about the rice cookery of the West, where rice plays a supporting role to other foods. In her subsequent travels she concentrated on rice usage and preparation. The results of her interest are the varied recipes that follow.

While rice is still the most important single food in Japan, adherence to the old "full" rice diet is lessening in the light of modern nutritional knowledge. On the other hand, rice consumption is increasing in Europe and the United States. It is Tomi Egami's belief that there is a need for more extensive information on rice cooking methods and recipes—hence this book. Add to this the fact that rice is inexpensive, that it can be used with every kind of food, and that it is nutritious. So why *not* a book of *Rice Recipes from Around the World?*

The Author

TOMI EGAMI, whose interest in cookery began at a very early age, was born in 1898 in Kyushu, which is in southern Japan, and was educated there. After her marriage to Iwao Egami, she pursued her hobby and completed courses in Japanese, Chinese, and Western cookery at the Tokyo Cooking School. In 1927 Mrs. Egami accompanied her husband, an army officer, to France, where she had the opportunity to study at the Cordon Bleu Cooking Academy from which she was graduated. This was followed by an intensive three-year study of French and English home cookery. Upon her return to Japan, she began to teach to an ever-enlarging group of enthusiastic students (among whom was the Imperial Princess Suganomiya). This led to her becoming head of the École de Cuisine Egami, which has its main school in central Tokyo and a flourishing branch on the outskirts of Japan's capital. Twenty thousand students have been graduated from these schools, and the current enrollment is 3,000. In addition to her schools, Mrs. Egami's busy schedule includes regular television and radio classes, lectures at women's group meetings, articles for magazines, as well as her extensive publications on Japanese, Chinese, and Western cookery.

Revisiting the United States and Europe in 1953, she received in Paris a special diploma from her alma mater, the famed Cordon Bleu. Since then Tomi Egami has made three trips abroad to teach and, at the same time, to enhance her own vast store of knowledge of food preparation. She has traveled extensively, and in every place she visited, she introduced or demonstrated her cooking skills. Her name must thus be counted among those of the great international cooks.

Working with Mrs. Egami in the production of this book were: Yoshikatsu Saeki, who is responsible for the admirable photographs; Masakazu Kuwata, whose design and art direction have contributed so much; and Lucille Evans, who provided editorial assistance and advice. Accessories and serving dishes are part of Tomi Egami's large collection.

Basic Recipes

Rice Cookers

A   B   C

To THE PEOPLE of Asia, especially to Japanese, Chinese, and Southeast Asians, rice is the staple food. In the Americas and Europe, rice is usually served as a side dish. Japanese and Koreans prefer the "soft" quality rice, while people in the other areas have a taste for the "dry" or "fluffy" rice. It is natural that the taste and use of rice differs by country, and, therefore, the cooking methods also vary to a certain degree. The best way to prepare rice is to cook it in accordance with the method common to the country where the recipe originated. For example, rice to be served with curry should be cooked to blend with curry, while rice for *sushi* should be prepared to suit its purpose. Rice should generally be cooked in a thick pan with a heavy cover. This requires some practice before you can perfect your technique. Automatic rice cookers (electric and gas), which are recent products, have simplified the process. The basic recipes listed in this book explain the cooking of rice with both utensils. Following are photographs of commonly used rice cookers.

D   E a   E b

A) An old Japanese cast-iron pot with a heavy wooden cover, which is still in use. It was originally designed for cooking rice over an **open fireplace.**

B) A thick aluminum pot with a curled edge to prevent rice from **boiling over.**

C) A thick European-style pot.

D) A round aluminum container with holes which is hung in boiling water. It rotates to cook rice.

E) An automatic electric cooker which has simplified the task of cooking rice. Adjustment of the rice and water– and a time switch–will give you the desired type of cooked rice at exactly the hour you wish to serve it. Adjustments can be made to cook rice together with vegetables and meat.

Pictured are two different types of automatic electric rice cookers: (a) is the regular type; (b) is a pressure-type cooker and therefore requires less time.

F) A Japanese-style rice steaming rack. This is placed on top of a regular iron pot to steam-cook rice.

G) A Chinese rice steamer.

F   G

Rice Cooking Methods

Basic Recipe (1)

THIS IS the usual Japanese way of cooking white rice.

Ingredients
   3 cups rice
   3½-4 cups water

Method
   Wash and drain rice until water becomes fairly clear, drain, and let stand for about an hour. Place rice in pan (A) or (B), add water, cover and cook over high heat until boiling point. Turn off heat and let stand for 3 minutes. Turn on heat to medium again, cook for about 15 minutes, then lower heat and continue to cook for another 10 minutes. Mix rice well to serve. Use automatic electric rice cookers for the same results. Use less water (3 ½ cups) for new rice, and more (4 cups) for regular rice.

Basic Recipe (2)

HERE IS the method for cooking rice slightly "harder" than above. Rice cooked this way is suited for Chinese dishes, Indian curry, and other Southeast Asian recipes. Each grain of the cooked rice should be fairly solid. The amount of water should be 10 to 20 percent less than in the previous recipe, varying with the thickness of the rice cooker and the quality of the rice. Use 3 cups of water for 3 cups of rice for the automatic electric rice cooker. Follow the same method of cooking as above.

Basic Recipe (3)

IN THIS method, the rice is sautéed before cooking.

Ingredients
   2 cups rice
   2 tbsps. butter (or 3 tbsps. salad oil)
   4 cups soup stock
   1 tsp. salt
   Dash of pepper

Method

Wash and drain rice (European or American rice can be used without washing). Melt butter in thick pan over medium or low heat, add rice and sauté for about 20 minutes until rice is slightly brown. Mix well while sautéing but do not crack rice grains. Add soup stock, salt, and pepper. Mix ingredients, cover, and cook over high heat until boiling point. Lower heat and continue to cook until liquid is absorbed (15 minutes). Turn off heat when rice begins to scorch. Mix and remove to another container.

Basic Recipe (4)

HERE THE rice is partially cooked by boiling and then finished by placing in the oven.

Ingredients

2 cups rice, washed and drained
6 cups water
2 tbsps. butter (or 2–3 tbsps. salad oil)
1 tsp. salt

Method

Boil water in a thick pan, add salt and rice. Mix, cover, and cook over high heat until boiling point. Lower heat and continue to cook for about 13 minutes, mixing occasionally. Drain and place rice in oven (360°F) for about 15 minutes to dry. Mix rice with fork a few times while in oven. If seasoning is to be added, do this prior to placing in the oven. If other ingredients are added at this time, use a slow to moderate oven (340°F) and leave rice in for about 30 minutes.

Basic Recipe (5)

RICE COOKED in the ball-shaped container (see rice cooker D) is suited for European recipes.
Release latch and open ball. Fill one side with washed rice, and close ball. Boil an adequate amount of water in a large pot, suspend in boiling water for 15 minutes; remove, put a dash of pepper in rice and place in oven for about 15 minutes to dry.

Basic Recipe (6)

BASIC RECIPES (3), (4), and (5) are best for non-Asian recipes.
To obtain similar results using an electric rice cooker, the following method is recommended:
Put 2 cups washed rice and 2 cups water in rice cooker and turn

on switch. When switch goes off, let stand for 3 minutes. Depending on the recipe, mix 2 tbsps. butter (or 2 tbsps. salad oil), 1 tsp. salt, and dash of pepper.

Basic Recipe (7)

RICE COOKED with sautéed onion.

Ingredients
    2 cups rice
    1/4 lb. onions, chopped
    3 tbsps. butter
    3 cups water
    1 tsp. salt
    Dash of pepper

Method
    Melt butter in pan, sauté onions until slightly brown, add rice and continue to sauté until rice is slightly brown. Add water and salt. Cover and cook over medium heat. When liquid is absorbed, lower heat and continue to cook for about 15 minutes or until rice starts to stick to the bottom of the pan. Sprinkle with pepper and mix well.

Basic Recipe (8)

JAPANESE-STYLE flavored rice.

Ingredients
    2 cups rice, washed and drained
    $2\frac{1}{3}$ cups water
    2 tsps. soy sauce
    1/2 tsp. salt

Method
    Put all of the ingredients in rice cooker and turn on switch. Let stand for 3 minutes after the switch goes off and mix well.
    Follow the cooking method for Basic Recipe (1) if an electric cooker is not used.

Basic Recipe (9)

JAPANESE-STYLE flavored rice with more ingredients, cooked by the same method as (8).

Ingredients
    2 cups rice, washed and drained
    2 cups water

1 ½ tbsps. vinegar
1/2 tsp. salt
2 tbsps. saké
1 ½ tbsps. sugar

Basic Recipe (10)

RICE COOKED with milk to be served to children or invalids.

Ingredients
2 cups rice, washed and drained
2 ½–3 cups milk
1 stalk leek, chopped
1 tsp. salt

Method
Cook in accordance with Basic Recipe (8).

Basic Recipe (11)

ANOTHER WAY of cooking rice is to steam it instead of boiling or baking. Glutinous rice is usually steamed. Large leaves (bamboo, lotus, banana, etc.) are often used to wrap rice for steaming.

Ingredients
2 cups glutinous rice, soaked in 4 cups of water overnight and drained.

Method
Spread rice evenly in steam cooker, make small holes in several places to allow steam to penetrate well, and cover. Boil lots of water in pan, place steam-cooker on top and steam over high heat for 40 minutes. Steam longer when cooking more rice. Pour a total 2 cups boiling water with 1 tsp. salt mixed in it over the rice three or four times while steaming.

Other Basic Recipes

Vinaigrette Dressing

Ingredients

3 tbsps. salad oil, 1 tbsp. vinegar, 1 tsp. salt, dash of pepper
Mix all ingredients lightly in a mixing bowl. Adjust quantity of salt in accordance with use.

Mayonnaise Dressing

Ingredients

1 egg yolk, 1 tbsp. vinegar, 1 tsp. mustard, 2/3 tsp. salt, dash of pepper
$1\frac{1}{4}$ cups salad oil
Place all ingredients except salad oil in mixing bowl and mix with beater. Add 1 tbsp. salad oil to mixture, mix well, then add another tbsp. salad oil, and mix. Repeat this process, increasing the amount of salad oil each time by 1/2 tbsp. (This means about 10 additions of oil.)

Roux

Ingredients

2 tbsps. butter, 2 tbsps. flour, $1-1\frac{1}{2}$ cups milk, $1-1\frac{1}{2}$ cups soup stock
Melt butter in saucepan, add flour, and heat, mixing con-
stantly. When roux is to be used to make white sauce, care must be taken not to brown mixture by overheating. On the other hand, in roux for *velouté* sauce (which needs slight coloring) and for brown sauce, the mixture is browned. When mixture is smooth, gradually add milk, soup stock, or liquids obtained by cooking meat or fish, starting with a small quantity and increasing it, while stirring constantly over low heat.

Steamed Cooked Champignons

Ingredients

1 lb. champignons, stems removed and washed
2–3 tbsps. white wine
2/3 tsp. salt
Dash of pepper
1 tsp. butter
4–5 drops lemon juice
Dash of thyme, bay leaves, parsley powder
Place all of the ingredients in a pan, cover tightly, and heat over low fire. When boiling point is reached, mix well and continue to cook for 5 minutes. Do not overcook.

Cold Dishes

SUSHI (WESTERN STYLE) (Japan)

SUSHI IS a Japanese favorite, but with a slight adaptation, using materials to suit the foreign taste, it is an ideal canapé.

Ingredients

3 cups rice
3 tbsps. wine vinegar
1⅔ tsps. salt
1/2 tsp. monosodium glutamate
2 thin slices boiled ham, cut in 1½″ × 2½″ pieces
6 oz. pickled herring, cut in 1½″ × 2½″ pieces
6 oz. salami, sliced thin, cut in 1½″ × 2½″ pieces
1/4 lb. smoked salmon, sliced thin, cut in 1½″ × 2½″ pieces
Omelet (mix lightly and cook in greased skillet until done 3 eggs, 2 tbsps. milk, 1/3 tsp. salt, and dash of pepper). Cut in 1½″ × 2½″ pieces.
8 boiled shrimp; remove heads, peel, cut in half lengthwise, and marinate for 30 minutes in mixture of: 1½ tbsps. vinegar, 1/2 tsp. salt, 2/3 tsp. sugar, and dash of monosodium glutamate
1 egg, mixed with dash of salt, 1/3 tsp. cornstarch, 1/2 tbsp. water and fried to form thin sheet. Cut in 1/2″ wide strips.
Mustard
Parsley sprigs for garnish

Utensils and Equipment

Rice cooker, bowls, skillet,

Method

Cook rice in accordance with basic recipe (1) on page 13. Mix vinegar, salt, and monosodium glutamate well in a bowl. Place rice in a large wooden bowl, pour in vinegar mixture and mix, using a wooden spatula. While mixing use a fan to cool the rice. Prepare ham, herring, salami, smoked salmon, egg omelet, and shrimp. Wet the palm of your right hand with water, take a handful of rice and ball it. Pick up a piece of ham with the left hand, apply a thin coat of mustard to it with right index finger. Place the rice ball in your right hand (see process illustration showing how to make a raw tuna sushi) on the ham. Cup your left hand, place right index and middle fingers on the rice and press to make the ball firm. Repeat process with ham, herring, salami, smoked salmon, shrimp, and omelet in the same manner. Use thin egg strips to tie around the salami and other stiff ingredients so that the top does not slide off. Serve on platter with sprigs of parsley as garnish.
Serves 8.

Variations

Use molds to shape rice cakes to suit ingredients to be used, such as pineapple, ham, shrimp, etc. as shown in the illustration. Use mustard between rice and ingredients if preferred and decorate with cherry, olive, sliced cucumber, or parsley.

ITALIAN SALAD (Italy)

THIS UNUSUAL SALAD made with rice, squid, and vegetables will prove a pleasant surprise to jaded appetites.

Ingredients
    1 cup rice
    1/3 tsp. salt
    3 tbsps. salad oil
    1 ½ tbsps. vinegar
    1 tsp. salt
    Dash of pepper
    1 lb. squid
    1/3 tsp. salt
    1/2 lb. celery, cut aslant in 1/8″ pieces, and sprinkled with salt
    1/8 lb. onions, sliced thin and sprinkled with salt
    1 bell pepper, halved. Remove seeds, dip in boiling water, and cut into 1/4″ strips
    8 ripe olives
    8 green olives
    1/2 lb. tomatoes, peeled, seeded, and cut into strips
    Salad dressing: 6 tbsps. salad oil, 2 tbsps. vinegar, 2 tsps. salt, dash of pepper

Utensils and Equipment
    Rice cooker, bowl, saucepan
Method
    Cook rice in accordance with basic recipe (4), (5), or (6) on page 14. Mix oil, vinegar, salt, and pepper in bowl, pour over hot rice. Mix well and cool. Boil squid in salt water, drain, and cut body in 1/8″ rings and legs in 1 ½″ lengths and cool. Prepare salad dressing, mix with rice and other ingredients except tomatoes and place in refrigerator for 2–3 hours. Stir occasionally.
    Add tomatoes and serve.
    Serves 4.
Caution: Mix rice with salad oil, vinegar, salt, and pepper when hot. Do not add tomato until shortly before serving.

ITALIAN SALAD

BEEF, EGGS AND WATERCRESS PLATTER
(France)

A HEARTY ARRANGEMENT of rice, roast beef, eggs, and watercress that has many purposes: a salad, a canapé, a first course.

Ingredients

10 oz. cold roast beef, cut in 1/2″ cubes
3 tbsps. salad oil
1 tbsp. vinegar
1 tsp. salt
Dash of pepper
3 tbsps. chopped onion
1 sprig parsley, chopped
1½ cups rice
2 tbsps. salad oil
2 tsps. vinegar
2/3 tsp. salt
Dash of pepper
3 eggs, boiled for 12 minutes (move occasionally to keep yolks centered) and cut into quarters
1/4 lb. watercress, washed
Salad dressing: 3 tbsps. salad oil, 1 tbsp. vinegar, 1 tsp. salt, dash of pepper

Utensils and Equipment

Large pot with cover, bowls

Method

Marinate roast beef for 4–5 hours in mixture of oil, vinegar, salt, pepper, chopped onion, and chopped parsley. Make preparations to cook rice in accordance with basic recipes (4), (5), or (6) on page 14. When boiling point is reached, place in an oven (340°) (20–25 minutes). Stir occasionally to absorb liquid. Mix with salad oil, vinegar, salt and pepper. Place rice in the center of the platter and arrange roast beef, eggs, and watercress decoratively around it. Serve salad dressing separately.

Serves 4.

Variations

Use ham, tomato, cucumber, lettuce, beets, or whatever ingredients suit your taste.

BEEF, EGGS AND WATERCRESS PLATTER

25

MUSSELS ITALIAN STYLE (Italy)

AN EXOTIC DISH combining mussels and red peppers in a mayonnaise sauce to serve with curry-flavored rice.

Ingredients
   2 tbsps. butter
   1 ½ cups rice
   2 tsps. curry powder
   3 cups soup stock
   Dash of salt and pepper
   2 ¼ lbs. small mussels (or clams), soaked in salt water for 3–4
      hours and washed
   1/2 cup white wine
   Dashes of thyme, parsley flakes and bay leaves
   2 pimentos, halved, seeds removed, parboiled in salt water,
      cooled, and cut into squares about the size of mussels
   5 tbsps. mayonnaise mixed with 1 tsp. mustard

Equipment and Utensils
   Heavy covered pot, saucepan with cover, bowl
Method
   Heat butter in heavy pot, add rice, and sauté until slightly
   brown. Heat curry powder slightly and add to rice with soup
   stock, salt and pepper. Then cook rice as in basic recipe (3)
   on page 13. Set aside and keep warm.
   Add wine, thyme, bay leaves, parsley flakes to mussels in
   covered pan and cook over medium heat. Remove mussels
   as they open and remove meat. Add peppers. Add mayonnaise and mustard, then add mussels to pimentos. Adjust
   taste by adding salt and pepper. Place mussels in the center
   of serving platter and surround with the cooked rice.
   Serves 4.

SAFFRON RISOTTO (Italy)

VARIOUS VEGETABLES with a hint of shrimp and ham mixed with saffron rice produce a colorful cold dish, useful for buffets or luncheons.

Ingredients
   1 ½ cups rice
   2 cups water
   1/2 tsp. saffron
   2 tbsps. chopped onions
   1 tsp. salt
   1/2 lb. shrimp, boiled in salt water, and peeled
   2 bell peppers, halved, seeds removed, dipped in boiling
      water, cooled, and cut into 1/4″ squares
   1/4 lb. celery, cleaned, cut into 1/4″ sticks, and salted
   10 green olives
   10 ripe olives
   1/2 lb. tomatoes, peeled, seeds removed and diced
   1 stalk leek, cut in 1/2″ sections
   1/4 lb. boiled ham, cut in 1/4″ cubes
   Salad dressing: 6 tbsps. salad oil, 2 tbsps. vinegar, 1 ½ tsps.
                  salt, dash of pepper

Utensils and Equipment
   Rice cooker, bowl
Method
   Place saffron, onion, and salt in water and boil. Add rice,
   mix well, and cook until rice is almost done (the degree may
   vary with taste, but do not overcook) and drain.
   Prepare salad dressing by mixing salad oil, vinegar, salt and
   pepper. Mix all ingredients in a salad bowl, pour dressing
   over and toss well.
   Serves 4.

MUSSELS ITALIAN STYLE

SAFFRON RISOTTO

27

RAISINS AND PINE NUTS IN GRAPE LEAVES (Turkey)

RAISINS AND PINE nuts mixed in rice, wrapped in salted grape leaves, and steam-cooked make unique—and wonderful—hot canapés.

Ingredients

3/4 cup salad oil
1 lb. onions, chopped
2 cups rice
1/8 lb. raisins, rinsed and drained
1/3 lb. pine nuts, rinsed and drained
3 cups water
2 sprigs thyme, 6″ (or 1/4 tsp. thyme powder)
2 sprigs mint, 6″
1½ tsps. salt
Dash of pepper
About 60 salted grape leaves (to salt grape leaves: Select large young leaves, wash and dry. Salt leaves and place them on top of each other in layers; weight down and let stand for three days. Use approximately 2 tbsps. of salt).

Utensils and Equipment

Skillet, bowl, covered pan

Method

Heat salad oil, sauté onions until slightly brown, add rice, and continue to heat until rice becomes slightly brown also. Add other ingredients except grape leaves. Bring to a boil over high heat, then lower heat to prevent boiling over. Continue to cook until liquid is absorbed. Then turn heat extremely low until rice cakes slightly at the bottom. Turn off heat and remove thyme and mint. Remove to bowl and let cool. Spread grape leaves bottom side up and place 1 tbsp. of rice mixture in center of each. Fold into squares (see illustration). Arrange tightly covered pans. Place cover directly over the contents, weigh it down with a light object, and cook over low heat. When the bottom layer starts to sizzle, pour in 1 tbsp. water and shake the pan slightly. Repeat this several times. Serve hot.

Serves 15.

Variations

Use cabbage or large spinach leaves instead of grape leaves.

RAISINS AND PINE NUTS IN GRAPE LEAVES

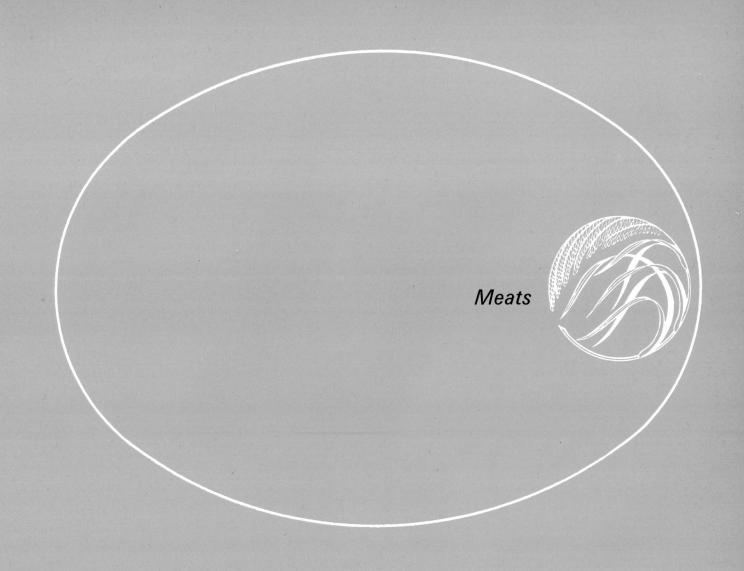

Meats

SUKIYAKI (Japan)

SUKIYAKI IS NOW internationally famous and rice is an integral part of this delicious meal. Western vegetables are included in this recipe to enhance its appeal.

Ingredients

Stock: 1 piece 4″×10″ kelp, 1/2 cup soy beans, 2½ cups water, 1 cup soy sauce, 3/4 cup sugar

2 bunches *shirataki*. Parboil, let stand for a while, drain, and cut in 3″ lengths.

1 head cauliflower (medium). Soak in 5 cups water, 1 tbsp. flour for 1 hour, wash, and break into 1″ square pieces.

1 lb. *shungiku*, pick soft parts only, and wash

3 stalks leek, washed, cut aslant 1/4″ wide

2 loaves roasted *tofu*, cut in 1¼″ cubes

1 lb. bamboo shoots, boiled or canned, cut in 1/8″ widths

3/4 lb. eggplant, cut in 1/4″ widths

1 lb. onions, cut in 1/4″ rings

2½ lbs. beef sirloin, sliced thin

1/4 lb. beef suet

3 cups rice

3⅓ cups water

Soy sauce

Sugar

Utensils and Equipment

Bowl, soup pot, rice cooker, electric skillet

Method

Soak kelp and soy beans in water for 7-8 hours. Add soy sauce and sugar, boil, and strain to make stock. Arrange *shirataki*, cauliflower, *shungiku*, leek, *tofu*, bamboo shoots, eggplant, onion, beef, and beef suet decoratively on large platter and have ready at the table. Cook rice in accordance with basic recipe (1) on page 13; keep warm. Heat skillet on the table, rub with suet, place some of the vegetables on the bottom, spread, put meat on top, and pour in stock. Cook lightly. Adjust taste by adding soy sauce and sugar. Repeat process with other ingredients. Serve rice and eat with sukiyaki. Dip sukiyaki in lightly beaten raw egg if desired. Serves 4.

Variation

Use stock obtained from boiling chicken instead of the listed stock. Use any other vegetables such as champignon, broccoli, asparagus, carrot, cabbage. Chicken or pork sukiyaki can be made with this recipe also.

SUKIYAKI

33

KOREAN BARBECUE

LEAN BEEF LOIN, sliced thin, marinated in a spicy sauce, and barbecued is a nice surprise for your next barbecue.

Ingredients
2 lbs. beef loin, sliced thin
Marinade: 2 cloves garlic, crushed; 1 red pepper, seeds removed, and chopped fine; 2 tbsps. sesame seeds, roasted and crushed; 3 tbsps. soy sauce; 2 tsps. sesame oil
2 cups rice
2¼ cups water

Utensils and Equipment
Charcoal brazier, grill, rice cooker
Method
Marinate beef for 10–12 hours. Cook rice in accordance with basic recipe (1) or (2), on page 13. Barbecue beef at the table to desired "doneness" and serve with hot rice. Oil grill to prevent beef from sticking.
Serves 4.
Variations
Use chicken or pork instead of beef. Use chopped leek or shallots instead of garlic in marinade.

DUKE OF ARGYLL'S TEA-TREE SOUP (China)

THE DUKE of Argyll's Tea-Tree Soup is considered a healthful drink. Once you try it, its unusual flavor and nutritional qualities will make it a family favorite.

Ingredients
5 Duke of Argyll's tea-tree branches, 12″ long, fresh leaves picked off, washed and dried; keep branches

1 lb. pork spareribs
1 tbsp. salad oil
9 cups water
1/4 lb. pork, cut in 2″ strips
1/2 tsp. salad oil
1/2 tsp. soy sauce
1/2 tsp. cornstarch
1½ tsps. salt
Dash of monosodium glutamate
2 eggs, beaten lightly and mixed with 1/4 tsp. salt
1½ cups rice
1¾ cups water

Utensils and Equipment
Soup pot, strainer, rice cooker
Method
Bend and bunch branches, and place in pot with pork spareribs, salad oil, and water. Bring to a boil over high heat. Lower heat to prevent boiling over and continue to cook until liquid is reduced to about 5 cups (1½ hours). Strain and reserve soup. Discard branches. Roll stripped pork in salad oil, soy sauce, and cornstarch. Heat soup, add pork strips, heat until cooked; season with salt and monosodium glutamate. Add Duke of Argyll's tea-tree leaves, mix in beaten eggs, and cook until eggs solidify. Cook rice in accordance with basic recipe (2) on page 13. Pour hot soup over half bowl of rice to serve. Serve hot.
Serves 4.
Variations
Use spinach instead of Duke of Argyll's tea-tree leaves. Use chicken bones for soup stock instead of pork.

KOREAN BARBECUE; DUKE OF ARGYLL'S TEA-TREE SOUP

ITALIAN RICE CROQUETTES (Italy)

AN ECONOMICAL, nutritious, and tasty lunch dish. Good for using up leftovers, too.

Ingredients
 4 cups water
 1 tsp. salt
 1½ cups rice
 2 tbsps. olive oil
 3 oz. onions, chopped
 1 oz. carrots, scraped and chopped
 2 oz. celery, chopped
 1/2 lb. beef round, chopped
 2½ oz. mushroom or fungi, chopped
 1/4 lb. tomatoes, peeled, seeded, and chopped
 1 tbsp. tomato puree
 1½ cups soup stock
 1 tsp. salt
 Dash of pepper, thyme, bay leaves, parsley, celery flakes
 8 pcs. Mozzarella cheese, 1/2″ square × 1″ long
 4 tbsps. flour
 1 egg, lightly beaten with 1 tbsp. water added
 2 oz. bread crumbs
 Oil for deep frying
 2 sprigs parsley

Utensils and Equipment
 Rice cooker, heavy pot, bowl, deep-fryer

Method
 Boil rice in slightly salted water and drain (see basic recipe #4 or #6 on page 14). Heat olive oil, sauté onion, carrots, celery until slightly brown. Add beef and mushroom, sauté, add tomatoes, and continue until tomatoes are soft. Add tomato puree, soup stock, salt, pepper, and spices, lower heat and cook for about 40 minutes more. Add rice to this mixture and mix well. Cool. Divide into eight equal portions and shape into balls (see process illustration). Place a piece of cheese in the center of each ball, roll in flour, dip in egg batter, roll in bread crumbs and deep fry in oil (340°) for about 2 minutes. Deep fry parsley in oil (285°) for 30 seconds. Place doilies or absorbent paper on platter, arrange croquettes, decorate with parsley, and serve hot.
 Serves 4.

Caution: Use soft quality rice to make the balling process easier or use beaten egg to make the rice grains stick together.

ITALIAN RICE
CROQUETTES

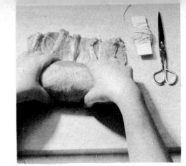

CURRIED VEAL ROAST (France)

A VERY NEW WAY to serve an old favorite. The delicate blandness of veal needs these exotic flavors to bring it to perfection.

Ingredients

2 lbs. veal rib roast (boned)
2 oz. butter
1¼ tsp. salt
Dash of pepper
1½ tsps. flour
2/3 cup water
2/3 cup wine
3 oz. butter
1/4 lb. onions, chopped
1½ cups rice
1½ tsps. curry powder
2½ cups soup stock
1 tsp. salt
Dash of pepper
2½ tbsps. butter
4 tomatoes (medium sized), top and bottom sliced off, and halved horizontally
Dash of salt and pepper
Sauce: 4 oz. butter, 2 tsps. curry powder, 1/2 cup white wine, 1/2 tsp. salt, 4 oz. heavy cream, dash of pepper
1 sprig parsley, chopped fine

Utensils and Equipment

Two heavy pots (one with cover), skillet

Method

Roll and tie veal (see process illustration) and slice in sections. Heat butter and brown tied veal on both sides, sprinkle with salt, pepper, and flour, continue to heat until slightly brown, add water and white wine, cover and cook over low heat, turning occasionally (about 30 minutes). Melt butter in thick pan, sauté onions, add rice, and continue until slightly brown. Add curry powder. When odor of curry becomes strong, add soup stock, salt and pepper. Mix well and cook in accordance with basic recipe (3) on page 13. Melt butter in skillet and fry tomatoes on both sides (cut ends) and sprinkle with salt and pepper. To make the sauce, melt butter, brown curry powder lightly, add white wine, stirring constantly, then add salt, cream, and pepper, and remove from heat when hot. Arrange rice in the center of a platter, surround with meat and tomatoes alternately. Sprinkle chopped parsley on tomatoes. Serve sauce separately.

Serves 4.

Suggestion

When cooking meat, decrease quantity of water and increase white wine if a more piquant flavor is desired.

CURRIED VEAL ROAST

39

PIEDMONTESE PORK CHOPS

THIS IS A NEW and unusually tasty way to serve an old favorite. Add a tart salad and a cool white wine for a special occasion.

Ingredients

2 tbsps. butter
1⅔ cups rice
3 oz. onion, chopped
2¾ cups soup stock
1 tbsp. tomato puree
2 oz. grated cheese
1 oz. butter
2 lbs. pork chops (4 chops)
3 tbsps. flour
2 tbsps. butter
Dash of salt and pepper
Sauce: 2 shallots, chopped, 2 garlic cloves crushed and
    chopped, 1/2 cup white wine, 3 tbsps. soup stock,
    1 tbsp. demiglace sauce, 1⅓ tsps. salt, dash of
    pepper, 1 tsp. cornstarch, dissolved in 1 tbsp. water,
    3/4 lbs. tomatoes (ripe and soft), peeled, seeded,
    and chopped

Utensils and Equipment

Heavy pot with cover, skillet, saucepan

Method

Melt butter in thick pan, sauté onion and rice until slightly brown. Add soup stock, tomato puree, salt and pepper, mix, cover, and cook rice in accordance with basic recipe (3) on page 13. Mix grated cheese and butter in rice and place in a low oven (340°), mixing occasionally, for about 15–20 minutes or until dry. Roll chops in flour. Heat butter in skillet and sauté chops on both sides for 15 minutes. Remove to plate, sprinkle with salt and pepper, and keep warm. Use same skillet, remove excess fat, and sauté shallot and garlic until slightly brown. Add wine, soup stock, demiglace sauce, salt and pepper. Transfer contents to a saucepan and heat over low heat until liquid is reduced to one-third. Add cornstarch to thicken, then tomatoes. Cover and cook over low heat for about 3 minutes. Serve rice on platter, arrange chops on top, and pour sauce over to serve.
Serves 4.

PIEDMONTESE PORK CHOPS

41

BURMESE COCONUT AND PORK CURRY
(Burma)

THIS BURMESE CURRY flavored with tamarind and served with coconut-milk rice is a unique addition to your curry recipe collection.

Ingredients

2¼ lbs. pork loin, cut 1/2″ thick, 2″ pieces
1/2 tsp. tumeric
1/2 tsp. anchovy paste
1 tbsp. grated ginger
1 tsp. paprika
1 tsp. chili powder
1 tsp. grated garlic
1 tbsp. fish sauce (or soy sauce)
3 oz. onions, grated
2/3 cup vegetable oil
Dash of salt
1 tbsp. salad oil
2 tbsps. chopped onion
1 tbsp. curry powder
2½ tsps. salt
1 tsp. tamarind, soaked in water and crushed (or dried apricot)
2 cups rice, washed and drained
2¼ cups coconut milk

Utensils and Equipment
Heavy pot with cover, skillet, rice cooker

Method
Place pork in a pan, rub with tumeric, anchovy paste, ginger, paprika, chili powder, garlic, fish sauce, and grated onions, and add vegetable oil and salt, cover and heat over medium heat. Add a little water to prevent scorching and cook until pork fat is tender (15 minutes). Heat salad oil in separate pan, sauté chopped onion until slightly brown, add curry powder, cooked pork, and season with salt and tamarind. Cook rice with coconut milk (see basic recipe #1 or #2 on page 13). Pour curry over rice to serve.
Serves 4.

Caution: Add a small quantity of water at a time to prevent curry from thinning out. Add a bit of sugar if tamarind is too sour.

BURMESE COCONUT AND PORK CURRY

GERMAN CURRY (Germany)

CURRY IS AN international favorite, and every country contributes its special touch. This is a typically German addition—heavy cream.

Ingredients
2 cups rice
2/3 tbsp. salt, dash of pepper, 1 tbsp. butter
2 tbsps. butter
1 lb. onions, sliced thin vertically
1½ tbsps. flour
1 tbsp. curry powder
4 cups soup stock
1⅓ tsps. salt
Dash of pepper
1/2 cup heavy cream
5 oz. sliced bacon

Utensils and Equipment
Heavy pot with cover, skillet, saucepan
Method
Cook rice in accordance with basic recipe (4), (5), or (6) on page 14, add butter, salt and pepper, mix, and place in oven to finish. Melt butter in skillet, sauté onion over low heat until soft. Add flour, curry powder, soup stock, salt and pepper, and continue to cook until mixture becomes thick. Then add cream, stir, and bring to a boil. Fry bacon crisply on both sides. Serve rice on a platter, pour curry sauce over it, and top with fried bacon. Serve hot. Serves 4.
Caution: Sauté onion over low heat well. Adjust amount of curry powder according to taste.
Variation
Use sausage or ham instead of bacon.

BACON AND OLIVE CASSEROLE (France)

AN EASY-TO-DO dish that can be prepared in advance is always a boon to the cook. This one will prove tempting to the most indifferent appetite.

Ingredients
1½ tbsps. olive oil
1⅔ cups rice
2 baby onions
4 oz. bacon, sliced and chopped
1/4 lb. green olives
5 pimentos, seeded and cut in 1″ squares
5 oz. sausage, cubed
1 tbsp. tomato puree
1/2 cup olive oil
2½ cups water
1/4 tsp. salt
10 peppercorns

Utensils and Equipment
Rice cooker
Method
Heat olive oil, sauté rice until slightly brown and add onion and bacon and continue to sauté. Add olives, pimentos, sausage, tomato puree, corn, olive oil, water, and salt. Cover, turn heat high, and cook until boiling point. Then lower heat and continue to cook until liquid is absorbed.
Serves 4.

GERMAN CURRY

BACON AND OLIVE CASSEROLE

IRANIAN KABOBS (Iran)

TRY THIS UNUSUAL combination at your next barbecue—a new and different twist.

Ingredients

1½ lbs. mutton, cut in 4, 2″×7″ strips
3/4 cup yogurt
1½ tsps. salt
Dash of pepper
1¼ tbsps. salad oil
3 tomatoes (medium), halved horizontally
Dash of salt and pepper
3 potatoes (medium), sliced thin, dipped into boiling water
  and drained
Oil for deep frying
Dash of salt and pepper
3⅓ cups water
2 cups rice, washed and drained
4 tbsps. butter
4 egg yolks

Utensils and Equipment

Four metal skewers (10″), mallet, grill, skillet, deep fryer, rice cooker

Method

Marinate mutton in yogurt and salt-pepper mixture for 2–3 hours. Stick mutton strips on skewers lengthwise, pound lightly on both sides (see process illustration), and barbecue over charcoal. Heat salad oil, fry tomatoes on both sides, and sprinkle with salt and pepper. Heat oil, deep-fry potato chips, and sprinkle with salt and pepper. Cook rice in accordance with basic recipe (2) or (4) on pages 13, 14. Serve rice on individual plates with egg yolk and butter and mix before eating. Serve mutton, potatoes, and tomato separately. Serve hot. Serves 4.

IRANIAN KABOBS

BEEF ROLLS (Italy)

A QUICKLY prepared but gourmet dish that will delight both family and friends.

Ingredients

1 tbsp. butter
1 cup rice
1/2 onion, chopped
3 tbsps. green peas
1 carrot (small), diced
2 cups water
1/3 tsp. salt
Dash of pepper
6 slices beef rump (1½ lbs., 6″×8″), seasoned with salt and pepper
Batter: 2 eggs, lightly beaten, mixed with 1/2 cup white wine, 7 tbsps. sifted flour and 7 tbsps. sifted cornstarch.
Vegetable oil for deep frying
5 oz. string beans
4 carrots (small), peeled and quartered
1 lemon, sliced or cut into 6 pieces vertically

Utensils and Equipment

Heavy pot with cover, skillet, saucepan

Method

Melt butter in pot and sauté onion and rice until slightly brown. Then add green peas, carrots, salt, pepper, and water, and cook in accordance with basic recipe (3) on page 13. When cooked, divide into six equal portions. Spread beef slices, place rice mixture on them (see process illustration), roll and stitch with thread to seal. Dip beef-rice roll in batter, heat deep fry oil (285°) and fry over high heat at 360°. Turn and fry for 3–4 minutes. Parboil string beans and carrots briefly, drain. Add a dash of salt to remaining batter, dip string beans and carrots and fry (320°) for about two minutes. Place beef rolls in center of platter, surround with vegetables and sliced lemon to serve. Serve hot.
Serves 6.

BEEF ROLLS

49

PORTUGUESE CASSEROLE (Portugal)

VEGETABLE FLAVORED RICE is served as an attractive mould surrounded by meats and vegetables, garnished with sausage, and is a meal in itself, equally suitable for dinner or lunch.

Ingredients
6 quarts water
1 chicken (2 lbs.), dressed and split in half
1/2 lb. pork spareribs
2½ lbs. beef
4 pork sausages (4″ length)
1 tbsp. salt
10 black peppercorns, crushed
4 frankfurters, cut into bite-size pieces
1 head kale, cut in 1/2″×2″ strips
1 carrot (large), peeled, and cut in 6 pieces vertically
1 turnip (medium), peeled, and cut in 6 pieces vertically
2 potatoes (medium), peeled, quartered, and soaked in water
12 oz. string beans, ends cut off, and tied in a bunch
3½ cups rice, washed and drained
2 pts. soup stock

Utensils and Equipment
Large soup pot, rice cooker, mould
Method
Boil water, put in chicken, pork, beef, pork sausage, salt, pepper and vegetables, and cook for 30 to 40 minutes. Remove chicken, pork and vegetables, and drain. Add frankfurters and boil for another 10 minutes. Use two pints of soup stock in rice cooker to cook rice. Cover, cook over high heat until boiling point. Lower heat and continue to cook for about 13 minutes. Butter inside of the mould, fill it with rice and invert on platter. Cut pork sausage into bite-size pieces, arrange on rice. Arrange kale around rice, cut chicken, pork and beef into sizes to match vegetables, untie string beans, and arrange on kale. Add seasoning to remaining soup stock to correct taste and serve separately as sauce. Serve hot. Serves 6.

PORTUGUESE CASSEROLE

Chicken

FRENCH CHICKEN CREOLE (France)

A WHOLE CHICKEN, cooked with wine and champignons and flavored with curry, is an impressive dish as well as a hearty meal.

Ingredients

1/2 lb. champignons, stems removed
2½ tbsps. white wine
1 tsp. butter
1/2 tsp. salt
Dash of pepper
4–5 drops lemon juice
Dash of thyme, bay leaves, parsley flakes
1 whole chicken (2½ lbs.), dressed
3 tbsps. salad oil
2 cups rice, washed and drained
2 shallots, chopped
3 oz. bacon, sliced, and cut in 1/4″ pieces
2 tsps. curry powder
4 cups soup stock
1/2 tsp. salt
Dash of pepper

Utensils and Equipment

Saucepan with cover, heavy pot with cover

Method

Put champignons, wine, butter, salt, pepper, lemon juice, and herbs in saucepan, cover and cook over low heat, mixing occasionally, for 3 minutes. Set aside. Heat 2 tbsps. of salad oil in heavy pot, put chicken in and brown on all sides. Sprinkle with salt and pepper and add the other tablespoon of salad oil, rice, shallots, and bacon, and brown. Add curry powder and sauté for a few minutes. Add soup stock, champignons, and liquid. Sprinkle with salt and pepper, and cook over high heat until liquid is absorbed. Then lower heat, cover, and continue to cook until rice is done. Place chicken in the center of the serving plate, arrange rice around it, and serve hot.

Serves 4.

Variations

Cut chicken into small pieces to serve with individual servings of rice.

FRENCH CHICKEN CREOLE

55

CHICKEN PAPRIKA (France)

CHICKEN DUSTED with paprika and baked in a special sauce proves a very easy-to-do and delicious dish.

Ingredients
  Sauce: 1½ tbsps. butter, 1½ tbsps. flour, 1½ cups soup stock, 1 tsp. salt, dash of pepper, 8 baby onions, halved
  2 tbsps. butter
  1 whole chicken (2½ lbs.), cleaned and cut in 8 pieces
  Dash of salt
  2 tsps. paprika
  2 tbsps. soup stock
  1/3 cup heavy cream
  1½ cups rice
  1½ tbsps. butter
  3 cups soup stock
  2/3 tsp. salt
  Dash of pepper

Utensils and Equipment
  Large, heavy pot (with cover), skillet, platters, rice cooker

Method
  To make sauce, melt butter, brown flour, and thin with soup stock. Season with salt and pepper (see recipe page 17) then add baby onions and cook over low heat until tender. Set aside and keep warm. Melt butter and sauté chicken in skillet until brown. Remove to platter and sprinkle with salt and paprika. Place chicken in pot with sauce, add 2 tbsps. soup stock, cover, place in a medium oven (360°), and bake for 30 minutes. Remove chicken and onions to platter. Add cream to the sauce, mix, and pour over chicken when serving. Melt butter, sauté rice until brown, then add soup stock, salt and pepper and cook rice (see basic recipe #3, page 13).
  Serve hot.
  Serves 4.
Caution: When sautéing chicken, move the pieces around so that they brown evenly, but turn sides only once to avoid breaking chicken skin.
Variations
  Instead of baking chicken in the oven, cook directly over heat if preferred. Add potatoes, carrots, and other vegetables as you prefer.

CHICKEN PAPRIKA

57

CHICKEN AU GRATIN (American Style)

CHICKEN AND vegetables in tomato sauce baked on rice and topped with cheese is a new and different answer to "what'll we have for Sunday brunch?"

Ingredients
  6 cups water
  1/2 lb. baby onions
  4 oz. carrots, cut into bite-size pieces
  1 lb. chicken, cut into bite-size pieces (with bones)
  Dash of thyme, bay leaves, and parsley flakes
  1/4 lb. champignons
  2 tbsps. white wine
  1/2 tsp. salt
  Dash of pepper
  1/2 tsp. butter
  Dash of lemon juice
  Dash of thyme, bay leaves, and parsley flakes
  Sauce: 2 tbsps. butter, 4 tbsps. flour, 4 tbsps. tomato puree, 2½ cups soup stock, liquid from cooking champignons, 1/2 tsp. salt, and dash of pepper
  1 cup rice
  1/2 tbsp. butter
  1/3 tsp. salt
  Dash of pepper
  2 tbsps. grated cheese (Gouda or process)

Utensils and Equipment
  Large, heavy pot, saucepans, rice cooker, casserole
Method
  Boil water in pot and put in onions, carrots, chicken, and spices. Cook for 20 minutes. Remove onions, carrots, and chicken, and save stock. Steam-cook champignons (see recipe on page 17). Make sauce by heating butter and add flour. Mix in tomato puree to form paste and thin with soup stock, adding seasonings and juice of champignons (see recipe on page 17). Add chicken and vegetables to sauce and cook over low heat, stirring occasionally until sauce thickens. Cook rice in accordance with basic recipe (4), (5), or (6) on page 14. Butter the inside of casserole, mix rice with butter, salt and pepper, put in casserole, and place in oven (340°). Stir occasionally to dry rice. Place chicken and vegetables cooked in sauce on top of rice, cover with grated cheese and place on upper rack of hot oven (445°) for about 20–25 minutes or until the surface browns slightly. Serves 4.
Caution: When boiling vegetables and chicken, remove onions and carrots before they become soft.
Variations
Use white sauce or cream sauce instead of tomato sauce.

CHICKEN AU GRATIN

59

INDIAN CURRY (India)

THIS IS a famous Indian recipe in which you prepare your own curry paste from scratch to make an authentic curry.

Ingredients

3 dried red peppers (1½ tsps. chili powder)
10 cardamon pods (1 tsp. cardamon powder)
1 stick tumeric, 2″ (1 tsp. tumeric powder)
1 stick cinnamon, 1″ × 2½″ (1 tsp. cinnamon powder)
1 tsp. coriander
1 tsp. carraway seeds
1/2 tsp. black pepper
15 cloves (1/2 tsp. clove powder)
4 litchi nuts, shelled
2/3 cup water
1/2 lb. margarine or butter
1 lb. onions, chopped
1 clove garlic, crushed, and chopped fine
1 whole chicken (2½–3 lb. broiler), cleaned and cut into 10–12 pieces with bones
Giblets from chicken, washed
1 lb. tomatoes, peeled, seeds removed, and cut into small pieces
1 cup yogurt (or sour cream)
2 tsps. salt
6 tbsps. margarine or butter
1/2 onion (small), sliced thin
1 litchi nut, shelled and crushed
1/2 tbsp. dill seeds
3 tbsps. yogurt (or sour cream)
2/3 tsp. salt
2 cups rice
2/3 cup green peas
4 cups water

Utensils and Equipment

Bowl, mortar, pestle, heavy pan with cover

Method

Wash spices, soak in water for 7–8 hours and drain. Crush with stone slab or mortar and pestle, adding water. Heat shortening and sauté onions and garlic until slightly brown. Add chicken and giblets and sauté until brown. Add tomatoes, mix well, and cook until tomatoes are soft. Add yogurt, salt, and crushed spices. Cover and cook over low heat, mixing occasionally until chicken meat is soft and becomes easily separable from bones.

To prepare rice, heat shortening, add onions and sauté until slightly brown, then add rice and sauté till slightly brown. Add litchi nuts, dill seeds, sour cream, salt, green peas, water, and cook rice over high heat for about 3 minutes or until liquid is absorbed, then lower heat and continue to cook for about 13 minutes or until rice sticks to pan. Serve rice and curry in separate dishes and serve hot.

Serves 4.

Caution

Be careful not to scorch onions and to cook curry over low heat. If using powdered spices, mix with lukewarm water to make paste.

INDIAN CURRY

61

TAIWAN CHICKEN (Taiwan)

CHICKEN SAUTÉED in sesame oil and saké will add a special flavor to that special occasion. Easy to fix, too!

Ingredients
2½ lbs. chicken with bone, cut in 1″ chunks
1 pc. fresh ginger, washed, and crushed without peeling skin
1½ cups saké
1½ cups water
1½ tsps. salt
Dash of monosodium glutamate
2 cups rice
3 cups water

Utensils and Equipment
Chinese-style frying pan (or large skillet), rice cooker

Method
Heat sesame oil and sauté chicken and ginger until slightly brown. Remove ginger and add saké and water. Cover and cook over low heat. Sprinkle with salt and monosodium glutamate when chicken becomes tender and continue to cook, stirring occasionally until juice thickens and chicken meat can be removed easily from the bones. Cook rice in accordance with basic recipe (1) or (2) on page 13. Arrange rice on a platter, pour chicken over it, and serve hot. Serves 4.

Caution: Sauté chicken well with sesame oil.

Variation
Use white wine instead of saké.

CHICKEN AND VEGETABLE SURPRISE (Japan)

RICE COOKED with chicken and vegetables and flavored with soy sauce is a favorite among children in Japan and will prove a favorite with all ages once it is tried.

Ingredients
3 cups rice, wash and drain about one hour prior to cooking
3 cups water
2 tbsps. soy sauce
2/3 tsp. salt
1½ tsps. sugar
3 oz. burdock, peeled and shredded
3 oz. carrots, peeled and shredded
1/4 lb. champignons, sliced
1/4 lb. chicken meat, cut in 2″ strips
1 oz. snow peas, ends picked off
1/4 tsp. salt
Dash of monosodium glutamate

Utensils and Equipment
Rice cooker, saucepan

Method
Put all ingredients except peas in rice cooker, mix well, and level surface. Cover and cook over high heat until boiling point is reached, turn heat to low and leave for two minutes. Turn heat up again for three minutes and gradually lower at three-minute intervals until fire is extremely low. Then leave for fifteen minutes. Boil peas briefly in water with a dash of salt, drain, and shred. Sprinkle with salt and monosodium glutamate. Garnish rice mixture with peas and serve hot.
Serves 4.

TAIWAN CHICKEN

**CHICKEN AND
VEGETABLE SURPRISE**

CHICKEN FRIED RICE (Chinese)

FRIED RICE mixed with chicken, shrimp, eggs, and vegetables —some commonplace, some exotic—is a meal-in-one-dish that is simple to prepare and delicious to eat.

Ingredients
1½ cups rice, washed and drained
1½ cups water
1/4 lb. chicken meat, diced
1 tbsp. saké (or white wine)
1 tbsp. soy sauce
1 tbsp. lard
1/4 lb. shrimp, heads removed, peeled, cleaned, and cut in 1/2″ pieces
Dash of salt and pepper
1 tbsp. lard
1/4 medium-sized onion, chopped
1 oz. carrots, boiled and diced
2 oz. bamboo shoots, boiled or canned, diced
2 dried mushrooms, soaked in water and cut in 1/4″ pieces
2 tbsps. green peas, canned or boiled
1 tbsp. lard
Dash of salt
1 tbsp. chopped leek
2 eggs, lightly beaten
3 tbsps. lard
1 head romaine lettuce
Salt and monosodium glutamate

Utensils and Equipment
Rice cooker, skillets

Method
Cook rice in accordance with basic recipe (2) on page 13 and cool. Marinate chicken in saké and soy sauce for about 20 minutes. Heat lard, sauté chicken for a minute. Drain on absorbent paper. Season shrimps and sauté in lard. Heat lard and sauté vegetables briefly over high heat and sprinkle with salt. Mix sautéed chicken, shrimps, and vegetables. Heat lard, sauté chopped leek briefly and pour in beaten eggs. Mix constantly to break egg into small pieces. Add cooled rice, use spatula to break rice chunks, mix well. Add chicken, shrimps, and vegetables. Mix ingredients well and sprinkle with salt and monosodium glutamate. Arrange leaves of romaine lettuce and serve hot.
Serves 4.

Caution: Cook rice with slightly less water so the grains are hard and can be separated easily. Use leftover rice.

Variation
Use pork or ham; substitute vegetables with your own favorites.

CHICKEN FRIED RICE

65

CHICKEN IN CREAM SAUCE (Portugal)

CHICKEN AND champignons in a rich sauce that will make anyone forget to count calories.

Ingredients
- 1/2 lb. champignons, stems removed
- 2½ tbsps. white wine
- 1 tsp. butter
- 1/2 tsp. salt
- Dash of pepper
- 5 drops lemon juice
- Dash of thyme, bay leaves, parsley flakes
- 2 tbsps. butter
- 4 oz. onions, chopped
- 1/2 lb. chicken meat, cut in bite-sized pieces
- 2½ tbsps. flour
- 2½ cups soup stock
- 1 tsp. salt
- Dash of pepper
- 1 cup heavy cream
- 1 cup rice
- 2 cups water
- 1/3 tsp. salt
- Dash of pepper
- 1½ tsps. butter

Utensils and Equipment
Saucepans, rice cooker

Method
Cook champignons with wine, butter, salt, pepper, lemon juice, and spices (see page 17). Set aside. Heat butter, brown onions, add chicken and sauté for 8 minutes, then add flour and brown. Gradually mix in soup stock, add cooked champignons, salt and pepper, and cook until juice thickens. Finish by adding cream. Boil rice, add salt, pepper, and butter, and place in oven to finish (see basic recipe #4 on page 14). Pour creamed chicken over rice and serve hot. Serves 4.

Variations
Use shrimp instead of chicken and make stock from shrimp heads and shells.

CHICKEN IN CREAM SAUCE

67

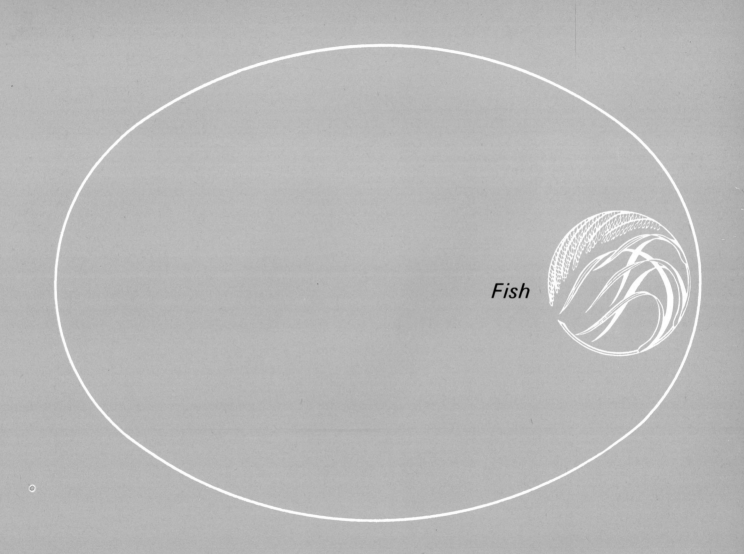

Fish

CREOLE FILET OF SOLE (France)

FILETS OF SOLE and sautéed bananas seem an odd combination with curried rice, but the delicate sweetness of the bananas combines well with the spices.

Ingredients
    2 filets of sole, sprinkled with salt and pepper
    4 tbsps. flour
    1 ⅔ tbsps. butter
    2 tbsps. salad oil
    2 cups rice
    5 cups water
    1 tbsp. curry powder
    2/3 tbsp. salt
    Dash of pepper
    1 tbsp. butter
    4 bananas, peeled, sliced lengthwise, then cut in half
    1 ½ tbsps. butter
    1 ½ tbsps. salad oil
    Dash of salt and pepper
    1 lemon, sliced or quartered

Utensils and Equipment
    Skillets, heavy pot with cover, casserole

Method
    Let seasoned sole stand for about 30 minutes and then dry with cloth. Cover filets with flour. Heat butter and salad oil in skillet and sauté filets on both sides. Boil 5 cups water, mix in curry powder and put rice in to boil for about 12 minutes. Remove from heat when rice is still half cooked and drain. Butter the inside of casserole, fill with rice, add butter, and sprinkle with salt and pepper. Place in oven (270 F) and heat for 15 - 20 minutes, mixing occasionally to absorb liquid evenly. Heat butter and salad oil in skillet and sauté bananas on both sides over medium heat. Then sprinkle with salt and pepper. Remove rice from casserole to center of serving platter and arrange sole, banana, and lemon slices around it.
    Serves 4.
Caution: Prepare bananas just before serving to retain scent and flavor.
Variation
    Substitute any other white meat fish filet for sole.

**CREOLE FILLET
OF SOLE**

CRAB PILAF FRENCH STYLE

CRABMEAT in a delicate white sauce, used as a filling for a
hollow rice mould, is a novel and delicious fish-day treat.

Ingredients
  2 crabs (3/4 lb. each)
  10 cups water
  1½ tbsps. salt
  3/4 lb. mushrooms
  3 tbsps. white wine
  Dash of thyme, bay leaves, parsley flakes
  1 tsp. butter
  2/3 tsp. salt
  Dash of pepper
  4–5 drops lemon juice
  2 tbsps. butter
  2½ tbsps. flour
  2½ cups milk
  2/3 tsps. salt
  Dash of pepper
  1/2 cup heavy cream
  1 egg yolk
  1½ cups rice
  1½ tbsps. butter
  3 cups soup stock
  2/3 tsps. salt
  Dash of pepper

Utensils and Equipment
  Saucepans: large, medium and small, pot with cover,
  casserole or mould

Method
  Boil crabs in water and salt. Cover pan with smaller lid to
  drop to water level and continue to boil for 30 minutes.
  Remove crabs, cool, and remove meat from body. Set crab
  claws aside. Remove stems from mushrooms and cook in
  white wine, butter, salt, pepper, lemon juice, and herbs
  (see page 17). Slice half the mushrooms thin (vertically).
  Melt butter over low heat, add flour gradually and stir to
  smooth paste. Add milk gradually to make thin white sauce.
  Continue to cook over low heat, add salt and pepper to suit
  taste, until sauce is well blended.
  Mix 1/3 of cream sauce with crabmeat and mushrooms.
  Add heavy cream to the remaining white sauce and stir over
  low heat until smooth. Remove from stove and quickly stir
  in egg yolk.
  Melt butter and brown rice. Add soup stock and cook (see
  basic recipe #3 on page 13). Pack rice in casserole (see
  process illustration), leaving center open. Place crabmeat
  mixture in opening and press firmly. Invert casserole on
  serving platter. Sauté remaining whole mushrooms in butter,
  salt and pepper until browned. Use as garnish along with
  crab claws around rice as in illustration. Serve sauce separately. Serve hot.
  Serves 4.
Caution: Pack the rice firmly in the casserole.
Variations
  Use canned shellfish (crab, shrimp, lobster) or chicken.

CRAB PILAF FRENCH STYLE

73

RICE AU GRATIN (Dutch)

FOR LUNCHEON, buffet or Sunday night supper, this unusual combination of flavors will bring demands for "More!"

Ingredients

1 cup rice
4 cups water
1 tbsp. butter
1/2 tsp. salt
Dash of pepper
1¼ lbs. cod, scaled, cleaned, head removed, cut into 3/4″ slices, and sprinkled with salt and pepper (save head for stock)
6 oz. shrimp, head and shell removed, drained and sprinkled with salt and pepper (save shells for stock)
2½ cups water
1/4 onion, sliced fine
1/4 carrot, sliced fine
Dash of thyme and bay leaves
8 medium-sized clams, soaked in salt water for 3–4 hours and washed clean (keep in shells)
2 tbsps. white wine
Dash of thyme, bay leaves, parsley flakes
1/2 tsp. butter
3 tbsps. white wine
1/2 lemon, squeezed
Dash of thyme, bay leaves, parsley flakes
3 tbsps. butter
4 tbsps. flour
2 cups soup stock
Dash of salt and pepper
1/2 cup heavy cream
3 tbsps. grated cheese

Utensils and Equipment

Rice cooker, soup pot, strainer, large casserole, pan with cover, heavy, shallow pan with cover

Method

Cook rice (refer to basic recipe #4 on page 14). Drain, add butter, salt and pepper and mix well. Butter a casserole, place rice in it and put in slow oven (250°). Turn occasionally and bake for about 20 minutes until rice is dry.

Place head of cod and shrimps and shrimp shells in pan, add 2½ cups water, onion, carrot and herbs and bring to a boil. Remove scum. Lower heat and cook for 20 minutes to make soup stock. Strain and reserve 2 cups.

Place clams in pan, sprinkle with white wine and herbs, cover tightly and steam until clams open. Remove clams as they open and discard shells. Strain liquid and add to soup stock. Melt butter in large shallow pan, remove from heat, and place cod and shrimp on bottom. Sprinkle with wine, lemon juice and herbs. Cover tightly and cook over low heat for 15 minutes.

Spread cod, shrimps, and clams evenly over the rice in casserole. Cover with white sauce made by heating butter, mixing with flour over low heat and stirring in gradually the soup stock until well blended and seasoned to taste—add heavy cream and mix briefly. Sprinkle casserole with grated cheese and place in hot oven (on upper rack) for about 20–25 minutes or until the cheese browns.

Serve hot.

Serves 4.

Caution: Do not overcook cod, shrimp, and clams. Remove when barely done. Do not make the white sauce too thick. Allow the sauce to seep into the rice.

RICE AU GRATIN

FISH FILLETS PAKISTANI STYLE

THIS SURPRISINGLY good dish uses curried fish fillets baked with rice and herbs, spices and milk.

Ingredients

1/4 lb. butter
1/2 lb. onions, sliced thin (vertically)
1 tbsp. cumin seed, soaked in 2 tbsps. water and crushed
1 tbsp. green pepper, minced
1 tbsp. fresh ginger, grated
4 small tomatoes, cut in half
1 tbsp. salt
1/3 tsp. tumeric powder
1/3 tsp. saffron
1½ tbsps. lime juice
1¼ lbs. white meat fish fillets, cut into 1″ pieces and sprinkled with salt, pepper, and lime juice
7 cups water
2 bay leaves
2 cloves
1/2″ × 3″ stick of cinnamon
1 tbsp. salt
2½ cups rice
1/6 tsp. tumeric
1/2 tsp. saffron mixed with:
    1/3 cup water
    7 mint leaves
    1 cup milk

Utensils and Equipment
2 heavy pots with covers, saucepan

Method
Melt butter and sauté onions until slightly brown. Set aside. Mix cumin seed, green pepper, ginger, tomatoes, and salt in pot and cook over low heat for 10 minutes. Add half of onions and tumeric-saffron mixture, stirring well. Add a few drops water, lime juice when liquid is absorbed. Add fish fillets and cook until liquid is absorbed, stirring occasionally.

Place bay leaves, cloves, cinnamon, salt in 7 cups water and bring to boil. Add rice, cover, and cook for 10–12 minutes until rice is half-cooked. Drain and remove condiments. Spread half of rice over cooked fish mixture, sprinkle with half the remaining tumeric-saffron mixture, and cover with mint leaves and browned onions. Place another layer of rice over this, sprinkle remaining tumeric-saffron mixture on the center. Pour milk around the edges. Cover and place in medium oven (300°) for 30–40 minutes until liquid is absorbed. Serve hot.

Serves 4.

Caution: Keep in oven until liquid is properly absorbed.

Variations
Substitute lobster for fish. Substitute lemon juice for lime juice.

FISH FILLETS PAKISTANI STYLE

77

TEN-DON (Japan)

A POPULAR LUNCH dish in Japan, this is made by putting *tempura* (batter-fried foods) over hot rice and pouring a special sauce over it.

Ingredients

  3 cups rice, washed and drained one hour prior to cooking
  3–3½ cups water
  4 prawns, peeled
  1/2 lb. squid. Separate head and legs, wash, peel thin skin, cut in 1½″ strips.
  1/8 lb. string beans, frenched
  1/8 lb. carrots, cut in thin 1½″ sticks
  1/4 lb. chicken meat, cut in 2″ strips
  1/4 lb. celery, cut in 1½″ sticks
  Sauce: 4 tbsps. saké; 2 tbsps. *mirin* (or sweet wine); 3 tbsps. soy sauce; 1 tbsp. sugar
  Batter: 1/2 egg; 8 tbsps. water; 1/2 cup flour; 1 tbsp. cornstarch; 1½ tbsps. rice flour; oil for deep frying

Utensils and Equipment

  Saucepans, rice cooker, deep-fryer, sifter, mixing bowls, absorbent paper

Method

Cook rice (see basic recipe #1 on page 13). Prepare sauce by heating saké and *mirin* over low heat to evaporate alcohol. Add soy and sugar. Remove from heat as soon as boiling point is reached. Set aside. Start heating oil before preparing batter. Beat egg lightly, mix with water, and gradually add sifted dry ingredients. Mix batter lightly, being careful not to have it sticky. When oil is hot (320°), dip prawns in batter and fry for 2–3 minutes. Remove to drain on absorbent paper. (This is prawn *tempura*.) Mix 1 tbsp. each of squid, carrots, and string beans in small bowl and pour in 1½ tbsps. batter. Mix again and drop into hot oil (see process illustration). Turn and fry for about 2 minutes. Repeat process and fry complete mixture. Repeat process with chicken and celery. Place rice in a large bowl, dip prawns, squid, chicken *tempura* in sauce briefly and then arrange attractively on the rice.

Pour 1 tbsp. sauce over ingredients. Serve hot.

Serves 4.

Caution: Press midsection of prawns firmly before dipping in batter to prevent curling when frying. If prawns are large, slit down center. Note: the batter should not be thick and it should splatter slightly when dropped in hot oil.

TEN-DON

MIXED SUSHI (Japan)

SUSHI—SHRIMP and vegetables mixed with sweet, vinegared rice—is not as well known outside Japan as *sukiyaki* and *tempura*, but it will prove a winner for canapés or snacks. Try it!

Ingredients

3 cups rice, washed and drained one hour prior to cooking
3 cups water
1/3 cup *mirin* (sweet saké) or sweet wine
1 sheet (4″×6″ square) dried kelp
Sauce: 3 tbsps. vinegar, 1¼ tsps. salt, 2½ tbsps. sugar, 1/2
         tsp. monosodium glutamate
1/2 lb. shrimp, cleaned and a bamboo skewer stuck through
         the back
1/3 tsp. salt
1½ tbsps. vinegar
2/3 tsp. salt
1 tsp. sugar
Dash of monosodium glutamate
4 mushrooms, dried (medium size), soaked in water and
         stems removed
1½ tbsps. soy sauce
1½ tbsps. *mirin*
2 tbsps. saké
1½ tsps. sugar
2½ oz. bamboo shoots, canned, cut into 1½″ strips
2 ft. strip dried gourd, soaked in salted water
Dash of salt
1/3 tsp. salt
1 tsp. sugar
1 oz. fresh peas, ends picked off, and parboiled
Dash of salt and monosodium glutamate
1 egg, lightly beaten and mixed with dash of salt, dash of
         monosodium glutamate, 1/3 tsp. cornstarch, 1/2 tbsp. water
1 tsp. salad oil
1 oz. pickled red ginger, shredded

Utensils and Equipment

Rice cooker, bowl, spatula, fan, saucepan

Method

Heat water, *mirin*, and kelp to boiling point, remove kelp and add rice. Cover and cook in accordance with basic recipe (1) on page 13. Let stand for about 3 minutes and place in large bowl. Mix sauce ingredients and pour over hot rice. Use wooden spatula to mix while fanning to cool. Boil shrimps in water with salt added. Cool, remove heads, peel shell, and quarter vertically. Soak in vinegar, salt, sugar, monosodium glutamate mixture for 30 minutes. Heat soy sauce, *mirin*, saké, and sugar to boiling point, then add mushroom. Lower heat and cook for 4–5 minutes. Remove mushroom from pan, cool, and shred. Save liquid. Parboil gourd until soft, and drain. Use mushroom liquid with salt and sugar to cook gourd and bamboo shoots over low heat for about 10 minutes. Drain and cut gourd in 1/8″ pieces. Parboil fresh peas and sprinkle with salt and monosodium glutamate. Heat oil and fry thin egg sheets, cool, and cut into strips. Mix rice well with cooked mushrooms, gourd, bamboo shoots, and peas. Garnish with egg and ginger to serve.

Serves 6.

Caution: Mix sauce into rice while hot.

MIXED SUSHI

81

VALENCIA PAELLA (Spain)

THIS COLORFUL Spanish-style recipe with its spicy flavor of saffron is a one-dish meal for family or guests.

Ingredients
- 1½ cups rice
- 2⅔ cups soup stock
- 3 tbsps. olive oil
- 3 oz. onion, chopped
- 2 shallots, chopped
- 1/4 tsp. saffron
- 1/4 lb. tomatoes, seeds removed and cut in 1/3" cubes
- 3 oz. ham, cut in 1/3" cubes
- 1½ tsps. salt
- Dash of pepper
- 1/2 lb. chicken, diced and seasoned with salt and pepper
- 3/4 lb. cod, scaled, cleaned, head removed, cut in 1" pieces, seasoned with salt and pepper
- 1/4 lb. shrimp, cleaned, peeled, leaving tails and last joint, heads removed, seasoned with salt and pepper
- 1/4 lb. squid, legs removed, skin peeled, and cut in 3/4" rings
- 1/3 lb. clams, soaked in salt water, washed, and left in shells
- 1 red pepper, seeds removed, cut in 1/4" strips

Utensils and Equipment
Large shallow pan, large soup pot

Method
Heat olive oil in large pan and sauté rice, onion, shallots, and saffron until rice turns slightly brown. Add tomato and ham and sauté for another few minutes.

Bring soup stock to a boil, add salt and pepper, sautéed rice mixture, and other ingredients, topping with red pepper. Cook uncovered over strong heat. When boiling point is reached, lower heat to prevent liquid from overflowing. When liquid is further absorbed, turn heat down to extreme low and cook until liquid is completely absorbed. Serve directly from the pan.

Serves 4.

Caution: The pan is flat and large and cooking is done without a cover, so move the pan around occasionally to be sure that it is heated evenly.

VALENCIA PAELLA

83

SPANISH MELANGE (France)

A FRENCH VARIATION of a popular Spanish dish, this is a hearty mixture of fish, shrimp, clams, chicken, and vegetables.

Ingredients

1/4 lb. shrimp, heads removed, peeled, cleaned, cut in 1/2″ pieces, and sprinkled with salt and pepper

1/4 lb. chicken meat, cubed (1/2″ cubes), sprinkled with salt and pepper

1/4 lb. onion, cut in 1/4″ squares

2 oz. carrots, diced

1/4 lb. champignons, stems removed, and quartered

1 oz. string beans, frenched

2 oz. tomatoes, peeled, seeds removed and diced

1 lb. clams with shells, soaked in salt water for 3–4 hours, and washed clean

1½ tbsps. butter

2 cups rice

3 cups soup stock

1½ tsps. salt

Dash of pepper

Utensils and Equipment

Heavy soup pot with cover, pan

Method

Heat butter, add rice and brown slightly. Then add all ingredients and cover. Cook over high heat until liquid is absorbed, then lower heat and continue to cook for about 15 minutes. Serve hot.

Serves 4.

SPANISH MELANGE

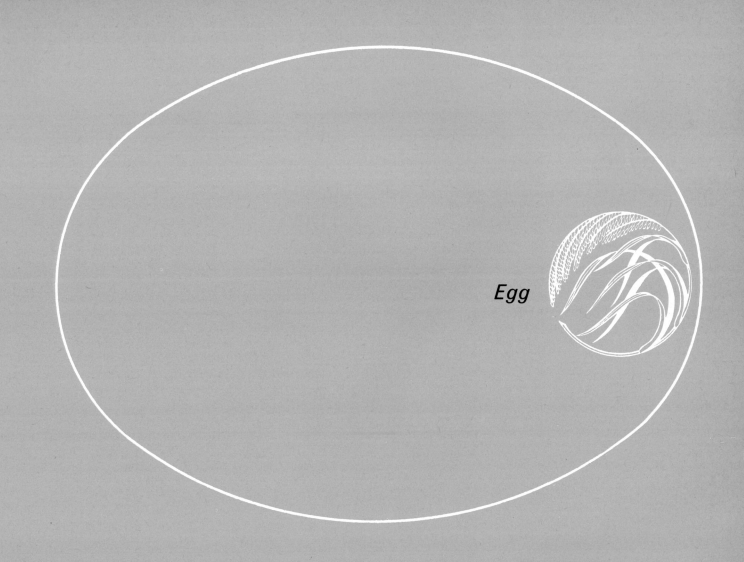

Egg

ALGERIAN OMELET (France)

SOMETHING NOVEL and special for Sunday breakfast or lunch any day is found in this ham and tomato omelet.

Ingredients

1⅓ tbsps. butter
1/4 lb. onions, chopped
1 cup rice
1/2 lb. ham, cut into 1/3″ cubes
1½ cups soup stock
Dash of salt and pepper
2 tbsps. butter
1/4 lb. onions, chopped
2 tbsps. flour
3/4 lb. tomatoes, peeled, seeds removed, and chopped
6 tbsps. tomato puree
4 cups soup stock
1 tsp. salt
Dash of pepper
12 eggs, beaten lightly
1/2 cup milk
2 tsps. salt
Dash of pepper
4 tbsps. butter

Utensils and Equipment
2 small saucepans, skillet

Method

Heat butter in pan, add onions, stir for a while and then add rice and sauté until slightly brown. Add ham, soup stock, salt, pepper, and cook, mixing ingredients well (see basic recipe #3 on page 13). To make tomato sauce, heat butter, add onions, and sauté over low heat until onions become soft. Add flour and cook until slightly brown. Add tomatoes and continue to sauté until soft, pour in tomato puree, and thin with soup stock. Add salt and cook over low heat until sauce is smooth and thick, then add pepper. Mix eggs, milk, salt and pepper well, and divide into four equal portions. Heat butter in skillet and pour in one portion of the egg mixture. Keep heat at medium and stir with fork a few times. When egg sheet starts to firm, place one quarter of the rice mixture in center and wrap with egg sheet. Repeat process until 4 omelets are prepared. Serve hot with sauce.
Serves 4.

ALGERIAN OMELET

89

HAM, EGGS AND EGGPLANT, SERBIAN STYLE (France)

FRIED HAM and eggs and rice cooked with eggplant is an exotic and hearty brunch.

Ingredients

3 tbsps. butter
1½ cups rice
1/3 lb. eggplant, cut in 1/3″ cubes
3 cups soup stock
1 tsp. salt
Dash of pepper
8 eggs
1 tsp. salt
Dash of pepper
Vegetable oil for deep frying
1 tbsp. butter
8 slices ham
1 sprig parsley, chopped fine
1½ tbsps. butter
1/8 lb. bacon, cut in 1/2″ squares
1/8 lb. onion, sliced thin
1/8 lb. carrots, sliced thin
2 tbsps. flour
1/2 lb. tomatoes, peeled, seeds removed, chopped
3 tbsps. tomato puree
2 cups soup stock
1/2 tsp. salt
Dash of pepper
Dash of thyme, bay leaves, parsley flakes

Utensils and Equipment

Rice cooker, mould, deep-fry pan, skillet, saucepan

Method

Heat butter in rice cooker, add rice, and sauté until slightly brown. Then add eggplant, soup stock, salt, pepper, mix well, and cook (see basic recipe #3 on page 13). Pack rice in mould. Keep warm. Heat deep-fry oil (340°) and drop one egg at a time into oil. Fry for 2–3 minutes, remove to absorbent paper, and sprinkle with salt and pepper. Keep warm. Heat butter and sauté ham on both sides. Invert rice mould on platter. Arrange ham around moulded rice, place an egg on each piece of ham and sprinkle with chopped parsley. To make tomato sauce, melt butter in skillet, add bacon, onion and carrots, and sauté over low heat until slightly brown. Add flour and continue to sauté until flour is slightly brown. Add tomato and cook until soft, then add tomato puree and thin with soup stock. Remove to saucepan, add spices and salt and continue to cook over low heat 30–40 minutes. Sprinkle pepper before removing from heat. Strain and serve separately with ham-egg-rice mixture.

Serves 4.

Caution: Soak eggplant in water for about 10 minutes prior to cooking. Select fresh eggs to prevent yolks from breaking when placed in oil.

HAM, EGGS AND EGGPLANT, SERBIAN STYLE

91

HAM AND EGGS (Japanese Style)

HAM AND SCRAMBLED eggs with milk and, of course, rice is a nourishing dish for children and invalids and a treat for anyone.

Ingredients
  3 cups rice (wash and drain one hour before cooking)
  3½–4 cups milk
  2 tbsps. shredded leek
  1⅔ tsps. salt
  Dash of pepper
  2 oz. ham, sliced and cut into 1/2″ squares
  3 eggs, beaten lightly
  1/3 tsp. salt
  Dash of pepper

Utensils and Equipment
  Rice cooker, skillet
Method
  Put rice, leek, milk, salt and pepper in rice cooker. Mix and level the top. Cover and cook rice (see basic recipes #1 and #8 on pages 13, 15). Add salt and pepper to eggs and scramble over medium heat. Break scrambled eggs in small pieces. When rice is cooked, mix in scrambled eggs and ham. Serve hot.
  Serves 6.

TRI-COLORED RICE (Japan)

A SIMPLE but colorful lunch dish that combines ground chicken, eggs, and green peas.

Ingredients
  3 cups rice
  3½ cups water
  1⅔ tsps. salt
  1/2 lb. ground chicken meat
  1 tbsp. water
  3 tbsps. saké (or white wine)
  2 tbsps. soy sauce
  2 tsps. sugar
  3 eggs, beaten well
  1/2 tsp. salt
  1 tsp. sugar
  Dash of monosodium glutamate
  1 cup green peas
  1 tbsp. salt
  2 tbsps. red pickled ginger, cut in thin strips

Utensils and Equipment
  Rice cooker, saucepan
Method
  Wash rice about one hour prior to cooking and drain. Add salt to water to cook rice (see basic recipe #1 on page 13). Put chicken, water, saké, soy sauce, and sugar in pan, mix well, and cook over medium heat. Stir well and cook until ground chicken meat breaks into small grains. Add salt, sugar, and monosodium glutamate to eggs and mix well. Heat over medium heat stirring well with chopsticks or fork. When egg mixture begins to firm, lower heat and mix rapidly to break into small pieces. Boil 4 cups of water, add salt, and boil green peas until soft. Drain and cool. Soak in salt water again later to expand skin and drain. Place a serving of rice in a bowl or plate and level surface. Place chicken, eggs, and green peas colorfully (see photo) and decorate with stripped ginger.
  Serves 6.

HAM AND EGGS

TRI-COLORED RICE

93

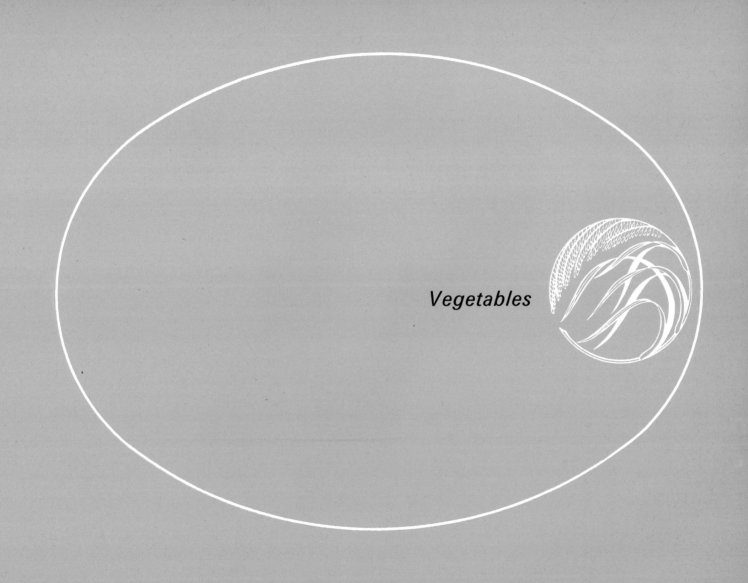

Vegetables

MUSHROOM RISOTTO (Italy)

THIS COMBINATION of such favorites as mushrooms or asparagus with rice is a delicious and noncaloric vegetable course.

Ingredients
  1½ tbsps. olive oil
  1/2 lb. mushrooms, stems removed and sliced thin vertically
  1½ tbsps. chopped onions
  1 clove garlic, chopped fine
  3 oz. bacon, sliced and cut in 1/4" squares
  1/3 tsp. salt
  Dash of pepper
  1/2 cup white wine
  2 cups rice
  3 cups liquid (water and juice from cooking mushrooms)

Utensils and Equipment
  Skillet, strainer, rice cooker
Method
Heat olive oil and sauté mushrooms, onions, and garlic. Add bacon and continue to sauté briefly. Sprinkle with salt and pepper, add white wine and cook over medium heat for approximately 2 minutes. Strain and keep liquid. Place rice in rice cooker and add liquid. Cover and cook over medium heat until liquid is absorbed, then lower heat and continue until rice sticks slightly to the bottom of the rice cooker. Let stand for about two minutes and then add cooked mushrooms and mix well. Serve hot. Serves 4.

ASPARAGUS RISOTTO

Ingredients
  3/4 lb. asparagus, soaked in 6 cups of water and 1½ tbsps. flour
  1½ tbsps. flour
  6 cups water
  1 tsp. salt
  4 tbsps. butter
  1/8 lb. ham, chopped
  1 clove garlic, chopped fine
  2/3 tsp. salt
  Dash of pepper
  2 cups rice
  3 cups soup stock

Utensils and Equipment
  Bowl, large saucepan, rice cooker
Method
Soak asparagus in flour-water solution for about 30 minutes. Remove and place in saucepan to boil with flour and salt added to water. Boil for approximately 12 minutes, drain, wash thoroughly, and cut into 3/4" lengths. Heat butter, brown rice, and sauté ham, garlic, and seasonings.
Add soup stock, cover, and cook rice in the same manner as the previous recipe.
Serves 4.

ASPARAGUS
RISOTTO

MUSHROOM
RISOTTO

STUFFED PEPPERS (Italy)

Bell peppers, stuffed with saffron-flavored rice, sprinkled with cheese and almonds and baked, will prove a new and different lunch or buffet treat.

Ingredients
 2 cups rice
 2 tbsps. salad oil
 3 oz. bacon, sliced and cut in 1/2″ squares
 2 shallots, chopped fine
 1/2 tsp. saffron, chopped fine
 4 cups soup stock
 2/3 tsp. salt
 Dash of pepper
 12 bell peppers, cut vertically on one side to form long cup
    (see illustration), seeds removed, and boiled in water with
    a dash of salt for 30 seconds
 6 tbsps. grated cheese
 1 oz. almonds, blanched and sliced thin

Utensils and Equipment
 Rice cooker, baking dish
Method
 Heat salad oil, add rice, and sauté until slightly brown. Add bacon, shallot, and saffron and continue to sauté for short while. Add soup stock, salt and pepper and cook rice (see basic recipe #3 on page 13).
 Stuff cooked rice in the bell peppers, sprinkle with cheese and almonds, and place in the top rack of a heated oven (445°). Bake until the top starts to brown. Serve hot.
 Serves 6.

MEXICAN CASSEROLE (Mexico)

This colorful mixture of saffron rice, corn, chicken and shrimp, with a variety of vegetables to add to its taste, makes a delicious one-dish meal.

Ingredients
 3 tbsps. salad oil
 1½ cups rice, soaked in slightly salted water for 30 minutes
    and drained
 1/5 tsp. saffron
 1/3 lb. carrots, peeled and diced
 1/2 lb. onions, peeled, and cut in 1/4″ squares
 1/3 lb. chicken meat, diced, sprinkled with salt and pepper,
    and let stand for 30 minutes
 1/3 lb. shrimp, heads removed, peeled, cleaned, diced, and
    seasoned with salt and pepper
 1½ cups corn
 1/2 cup green peas
 2 tbsps. tomato puree
 2¾ cup soup stock
 2 tsps. salt
 Dash of chili powder

Utensils and Equipment
 Heavy soup pot with cover
Method
 Heat oil in pan and sauté rice until slightly brown, add saffron, carrots, onion, chicken, shrimp, corn, and green peas and continue to sauté for a few minutes. Add tomato puree, soup stock, salt, and chili powder. Cover and cook over strong heat until contents boil, then lower heat. When liquid is absorbed, reduce heat further and continue to cook until rice starts to stick to the bottom. Serve hot.
 Serves 4.

STUFFED PEPPERS

MEXICAN CASSEROLE

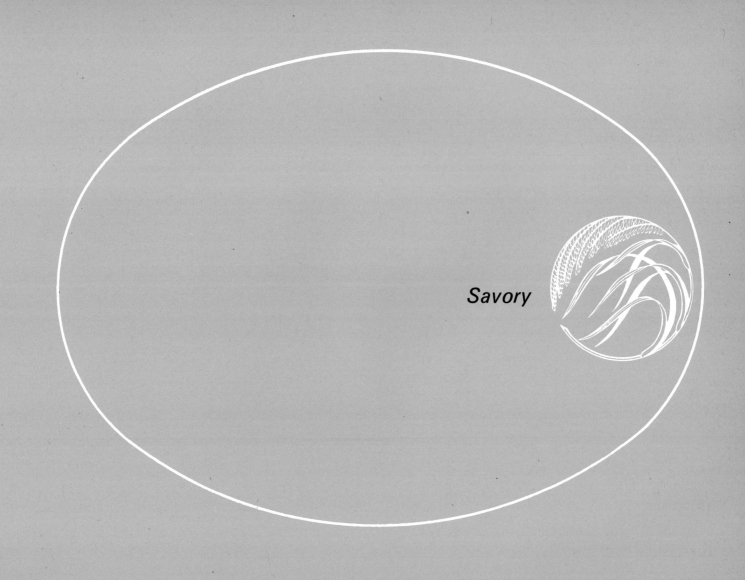

Savory

IMPERIAL MOULD (France)

THIS RICH moulded dessert has everything—flavor, nourishment and eye appeal. It originated in Bavaria.

Ingredients
  2/3 cup rice
  6 cups water
  2½ cups milk
  1/2 cup sugar
  1/2 oz. gelatin, softened in water
  4 egg yolks, beaten
  1 cup heavy cream
  Dash of vanilla
  8 plums
  1 cherry
  2 oz. angelica
  1 oz. lemon peel
  5 oz. cranberry jelly
  3 tbsps. water
  1/3 tsp. cornstarch, dissolved in 1 tsp. water
  Kirsch

Utensils and Equipment
  Heavy pot, bowl, double boiler, egg beater, saucepan

Method
  Boil rice for 12–13 minutes, drain, and place in 300° oven to dry. Put sugar and gelatin in milk and stir to dissolve. Put egg yolks in top of double boiler, stir in milk solution briskly, and heat. Stir slowly and heat until mixture thickens. Then place top pan in water to cool, stirring constantly. Whip cream until thickness is similar to other mixture and mix the two together. Add cooked rice and vanilla. Place pan in water again and stir to cool. Slice plum, cherry, angelica, and lemon peel in appropriate shapes for decoration (see illustration). Wet the inside of mould, arrange fruit on bottom and sides, slowly pour in mixture, and chill. Put cranberry jelly in saucepan, add water, and heat, stirring well. When this is cooked, add cornstarch paste to make sauce and cool. Invert mould on a chilled serving plate, pour cranberry sauce around it, and sprinkle with kirsch to serve.
  Serves 6.
Caution: Remember that fruit on sides of the mould will show when served. Make layers of the decorations by dividing the fruit and pouring in layers of the mixture one at a time.

SABANET (Pakistan)

SAFFRON, tumeric, cinnamon, and other spices added to nuts, raisins, and rice result in a dessert that will soon become a family favorite.

Ingredients
  2 cups rice
  8 cups water
  1 cup water
  2 cups sugar
  1/4 tsp. tumeric
  1 tsp. saffron
  6 tbsps. butter
  1 cinnamon stick (1/2″ wide and 4″ long)
  6 cardamon seeds
  2 bay leaves
  15 almonds, salted and hot water poured over to peel, and
    sliced thin
  1 tbsp. raisins

Utensils and Equipment
  Saucepan, large pot, casserole (or baking dish)
Method
  Boil rice in eight cups of water until half cooked and drain. Heat water, add sugar, tumeric, and saffron and mix to dissolve. Melt butter, add cinnamon, cardamon, bay leaves, then half-cooked rice and sugar solution. Cook over medium heat until liquid is absorbed. Add almonds and raisins, mix well, place in casserole or baking dish, and put in 300° oven. Bake for about 30 minutes, stirring occasionally. Remove large pieces of cinnamon, bay leaves, etc. and serve hot.
  Serves 6.

KIRSCH CAKES (Switzerland)

KIRSCH, a famed Swiss product, provides the flavor and scent of these delicate rice cakes.

Ingredients
  1 ½ cups rice
  8 cups water
  1 tbsp. butter
  1 cup milk
  1/4 cup sugar
  Dash of vanilla
  6 cherries
  6 plums, pitted, and halved
  2/3 cup water
  3 tbsps. sugar
  1 tsp. cornstarch dissolved in 1 tbsp. water
  2–3 tbsps. kirsch

Utensils and Equipment
  Heavy pan with cover, six small moulds
Method
  Boil rice in 8 cups water for 12–13 minutes, drain, and place in oven to dry (see basic recipes #4, 5, and 6 on page 14). Remove rice from oven, add butter, milk, sugar, and vanilla. Mix well, cover, and place on low heat for 10 minutes. Wet the inside of moulds, fill them with cooked rice, and then invert on a serving platter. Place a cherry in the middle of each, arrange plum halves on sides and chill. Heat water, add sugar, and dissolve. Mix in cornstarch-water solution to thicken. Remove from heat and cool. Mix in kirsch and when topping is cool pour over chilled cake to serve.
  Serves 6.
Variation
  Decorate with any other fruit.

KIRSCH CAKES

SABANET

105

NIGHTINGALE ROLLS (Japan)

SWEET GREEN PEA paste wrapped in cooked rice jelly-roll style is an interesting new dessert that is simple to prepare.

Ingredients
    1 cup glutinous rice, washed and soaked in 3 cups of water
        overnight
    4/5 cup water
    1 tbsp. sugar
    2½ cups green peas
    5/8 cup sugar
    1/4 tsp. salt
    1 tbsp. rice powder

Utensils and Equipment
    Rice cooker, bowls, saucepans, sieve, pastry board, knife
Method
    Drain rice, put in cooker and add 4/5 cup water. Cover and cook (see basic recipe #1 on page 13). Add sugar to rice as soon as heat is turned off, mix lightly, cover again and let stand for 5 minutes. Then remove to another container to cool. Boil green peas, adding 1/4 tsp. salt. When green peas are cooked, drain, remove to a bowl, crush thoroughly, and push through a sieve. Put crushed peas in a pan, add sugar and salt, and cook over low heat for 10–15 minutes, mixing well. Cook until paste becomes the consistency of jelly and then cool. Sprinkle rice powder on a dry pastry board, take half of the cooked rice, wet the tip of your fingers and spread rice to about a 6″ square. Place half of the paste on the rice and spread evenly. Use edge of a knife and roll the rice and paste like a jelly roll (see process illustration). Repeat process with remaining half. Cut roll in 3/4″ lengths and arrange them on pretty platter.
Serves 4.
Variation
Use red bean paste instead of green peas.

NIGHTINGALE ROLLS

107

KO YEH FAN (Chinese)

ANOTHER "savoury," which combines rice with shrimp, pork, lotus seeds, chestnuts, raisins, bamboo shoots, and mushrooms, is wrapped in a lotus leaf. A Chinese favorite for tea, it makes an exotic addition to the cocktail hour.

Ingredients
  2 cups glutinous rice, soaked in water overnight and drained
  1/2 cup water
  1 tbsp. soy sauce
  1/2 tsp. salt
  1 tbsp. sugar
  2 tbsps. saké
  1/4 lb. chestnuts, boiled, peeled, in 1/4″ cubes
  1½ oz. lotus seeds, boiled
  1½ oz. raisins
  2 oz. bamboo shoots, canned or boiled, in 1/4″ cubes
  2 medium-sized dried mushrooms, soaked in water, cut into 1/4″ squares
  3 oz. pork, cubed, seasoned with salt and pepper
  1/4 lb. shrimp, peeled, heads removed, cleaned, cut into 1/4″ pieces, seasoned with salt and pepper
  1 large lotus leaf, dried

Utensils and Equipment
  Bowls, steamer
Method
  Soak rice in water, soy sauce, salt, sugar, and saké, and leave for 1½–2 hours. Drain and keep liquid. Place rice in steamer lined with gauze. Cover and steam over strong heat, spraying liquid over rice occasionally, for 30 minutes or until 90 percent done. Mix rice with chestnuts, lotus seeds, raisins, bamboo shoots, mushrooms, pork, and shrimp. Place lotus leaf in bowl (see process illustration), fill with mixture and wrap. Place bowl in steamer and steam over high heat for 30 minutes. Remove to serving platter, slice top off and serve ingredients with spoon. Serve hot.
  Serves 6.
Caution: Soak rice in water overnight to soften sufficiently.
Variation
  Use chicken instead of pork or use fresh mushrooms in season. Use banana leaf or aluminum foil instead of lotus leaf.

KO YEH FAN

109

LEMPER MENADO (Indonesia)

THE NORTHERN Celebes contribute this flavorsome combination which includes coconut (of course). Add a crisp salad for a pleasant light meal.

Ingredients

2 cups glutinous rice, washed and soaked in water overnight
1 cup coconut milk
1½ tbsps. coconut oil
2 shallots (small), chopped fine
1 red pepper, chopped fine
4 oz. chicken meat, ground
1 tomato (medium), peeled, seeded, and chopped
2/3 tsp. salt
1 stalk lemongrass, cut in 2″ lengths
Banana leaves (12 6″ squares and 12 4″ squares)

Utensils and Equipment

Steamer, bowl, saucepan, toothpicks

Method

Drain rice and steam over strong heat for 15 minutes. Remove rice to a bowl, mix with coconut milk, and let stand for about 5 minutes. Place in steamer again and steam over strong heat for 30 minutes. Heat coconut oil, sauté shallot and red pepper briefly, add ground chicken meat, tomato and a bit of water, and flavor with salt and lemongrass. Sauté until chicken meat is done. Remove lemongrass. Spread out 1 large banana leaf and place a smaller leaf in the center. Place portion of rice on small leaf and put 1/12 of mixture on rice. Wrap (see process illustration), using toothpicks to secure both ends of the leaf packet. Place in the steamer again to heat. Serve hot. Serves 4.

Variation

Instead of chicken use fish fillet boiled in salt water.

LEMPER MENADO

RED RICE WITH CHESTNUTS (Japan)

IT IS CUSTOMARY in Japan to serve red rice on festive occasions, such as birthdays and weddings. Chestnuts add a unique flavor to this special dessert.

Ingredients
- 4 cups glutinous rice, washed and soaked in 8 cups of water overnight
- 1/2 cup red beans, washed and soaked in 2 cups of water overnight
- 1/2 lb. chestnuts, soaked in water overnight, peeled, and quartered
- Dash of red coloring
- 1 tsp. salt
- 1 tbsp. black sesame seeds
- 1/2 tbsp. salt

Utensils and Equipment
- Bowls, saucepan, steamer

Method
Mix red food coloring with soaked rice, let stand for 1 hour, and drain. Boil red beans for about 30 minutes and drain. Mix rice, cooked red beans, and chestnuts. Place in steamer and steam over high heat for 40–50 minutes. Make small holes in rice so that steam gets through well, and spray hot salt water (1 tsp. of salt in 2 cups of water) over rice 3–4 times while steaming. Mix salt and black sesame seeds, roast over low heat, mixing well, and sprinkle over rice when serving. Serve hot or cold.
Serves 6

Variation
Use water in which red beans were boiled to spray rice while steaming instead of red coloring.

RICE CAKES WRAPPED IN BAMBOO LEAVES (Japan)

AN ESPECIALLY attractive dessert that appeals to all those with a sweet tooth. It is nutritious as well.

Ingredients
- 2½ cups glutinous rice
- 2½ cups water
- 1¼ tsps. baking soda
- Sauce: 1 tbsp. soy sauce; 1 tsp. sugar, mixed together
- 2 tbsps. ground soy beans, 1 tbsp. sugar, 1/6 tsp. salt, mixed together
- 40 bamboo leaves

Utensils and Equipment
- Steamer

Method
Soak rice in water/baking-soda solution overnight, then drain. Wash the bamboo leaves, make a cone, fill with 2 tsps. rice, and tuck in end to secure (see process illustration). Boil adequate quantity of water in steamer, put in wrapped rice, and steam over high heat 40 minutes. Peel bamboo leaf wrapping off and dip into sauce or roll in ground soy bean, sugar, and salt to eat. Serve hot or cold.
Serves 4

RED RICE WITH CHESTNUTS; RICE CAKES WRAPPED IN BAMBOO LEAVES

CHESTNUT BALLS (Chinese)

STEAMED CHESTNUTS with ground pork and rice make a delicious final course – not unlike the British "savoury."

Ingredients
 1/2 cup glutinous rice, washed and soaked in water overnight
 3/4 lb. ground pork
 1/3 stalk leek, chopped
 1/2 tsp. grated fresh ginger
 1 tbsp. saké
 1 tsp. salt
 Dash of monosodium glutamate
 5 sweet canned chestnuts, quartered
 Soy sauce
 Mustard

Utensils and Equipment
 Bowls, sieve, steamer, plate

Method
 Mix ground pork with chopped leek, ginger, saké, salt, and monosodium glutamate well with hands and divide into 20 equal portions. Wrap chestnuts with ground pork mixture. Form into small balls. Drain rice and dry with cloth. Spread rice on a plate, roll chestnut-ground pork balls in rice and coat evenly. Spread cloth in a steamer and place balls on it. Steam for 15–20 minutes over medium heat. Serve hot with soy sauce and mustard.
 Serves 4.

Caution: If it is not possible to soak rice overnight, soak it in lukewarm water and leave in the sun to soften. The flavor of the ground pork will be lost if rice is not softened and more time is required to steam the rice balls.

Variation
 Use cooked sweet potatoes instead of chestnuts.

CHESTNUT BALLS
115

REGENCE SALAD (Italy)

THE COMBINATION of chicken meat, cucumber, mushrooms, and rice is an unusual and refreshing treat.

Ingredients
  5 cups water
  1 onion (small), sliced thin
  1 carrot (small), sliced thin
  Pinch of thyme, bay leaf, parsley flakes
  3/4 lb. chicken
  Salad dressing: 4 ½ tbsps. salad oil, 1 ½ tbsps. vinegar,
    1 ½ tsps. salt, dash of pepper
  1/4 lb. mushrooms
  Dash of salt and pepper
  1 ½ tbsps. white wine
  1/4 tsp. butter
  2 tsps. lemon juice
  Pinch of thyme, bay leaf, parsley flakes
  1/4 lb. cucumber, cut in 1 ½″ sticks and sprinkled with salt
  1 sprig parsley, chopped fine
  1 shallot, chopped fine
  1 cup rice

Utensils and Equipment
  Rice cooker, saucepans, soup pot, bowls
Method
  Boil water, add onion, carrots, spices, and chicken, and cook for 20 minutes. Bone chicken and tear into small strips (about the thickness of a pencil). Sprinkle with salad dressing and mix well. Salt and pepper mushrooms and cook with white wine, butter, lemon juice, thyme, bay leaf, and parsley flakes (see page 17). Slice mushrooms thin lengthwise, sprinkle with salad dressing and mix well. Squeeze sliced cucumbers and mix with salad dressing. Mix chopped parsley and shallot together well. Cook rice in accordance with basic recipe (3), (4), or (5) on pages 13 and 14; place in oven to dry and mix with salad dressing. Mould rice platter and level the surface. Cover one-half of the surface with chicken, mushrooms, and cucumbers, and the remaining half with chopped parsley and shallot.
Serve cold.
Serves 4.

CARMEN SALAD (Spain)

A COLORFUL salad topped with red (tomato), yellow (eggs), and green (peas).

Ingredients
  1 ½ cups rice
  1/8 lb. boiled ham, sliced thin and cut in 1/4″ squares
  3 tbsps. canned green peas, rinsed in boiling water
  Salad dressing (A): 3 tbsps. salad oil, 1 tbsp. vinegar, 1 tsp. salt, dash of pepper

1/2 lb. tomatoes, sliced in 1/8″ pieces

3 eggs, boiled for 12 minutes (move occasionally to keep yolk in center) and sliced thin

1 ½ tbsps. canned green peas, rinsed in boiling water

Salad dressing (B): 2 tbsps. salad oil, 2 tsps. vinegar, 2/3 tsp. salt, dash of pepper

Utensils and Equipment

Rice cooker (or pot with cover), bowl, egg slicer

Method

Cook rice in accordance with basic recipe (3), (4), or (5) on pages 13 and 14. Cool rice and mix well with ham, green peas, and salad dressing (A). Place rice mixture on platter, level surface and arrange tomato slices, eggs, green peas in that order from the outside to cover entire surface. Pour salad dressing (B) over the salad and serve.

Serves 4.

Variation

Use macaroni instead of rice.

SPICED CHICKEN (Spain)

SAUTÉ CHICKEN with olive oil, add spice, and cook with rice. The result: an exotic Spanish dish.

Ingredients

2¼ lb. chicken (broiler), dressed, rubbed with lemon, and quartered

1/4 cup olive oil

1 bell pepper, chopped fine

2 oz. onion, chopped fine

1 clove garlic, chopped fine

3/4 cup olive oil

3 tomatoes, medium size, peeled, seeds removed, and chopped

1 cup rice, washed and drained

2 cups soup stock

3/4 tsp. cayenne pepper

1/5 tsp. saffron powder

Dash of salt and pepper

5 oz. string beans: cut ends and parboil

3 bell peppers: cut in 1/4″ width rings and parboil slightly

1/2 tsp. olive oil

Utensils and Equipment

Saucepans, rice cooker

Method

Heat olive oil in flat saucepan and sauté chicken until slightly brown, remove to a separate plate, and salt and pepper. Use the same saucepan to sauté briefly the bell pepper, onion, and garlic. Then put chicken back in the saucepan, pour olive oil over it, cover pan and sauté for 15 minutes more. Then add tomato, soup stock, rice, cayenne pepper, saffron, salt, and pepper; cover, turn heat high and cook until boiling point, then lower heat and cook for another 20 minutes or until chicken meat is soft and easily separates from bones. Heat olive oil, sauté bell pepper and string

beans, and sprinkle with salt and pepper. Garnish cooked rice and chicken with sautéed bell pepper and string beans to serve.
Serves 4.

SHRIMP RISOTTO (Italy)

RICE COOKED with shrimps and saffron, then decorated with tomatoes, greens, and egg white, is a colorful and delicious meal.

Ingredients
    3 cups rice, washed and drained
    3–3 ½ cups water
    7 oz. shrimp, peeled and cleaned
    1/3 tsp. saffron
    2 tsps. salt
    Dash of pepper
    1 egg, boiled hard
    10 shallot greens, cut in 1/4″ strips
    6 tomatoes (small), quartered

Utensils and Equipment
    Saucepan, rice cooker
Method
    Put rice, water, shrimps, saffron, salt, and pepper in rice cooker, and cook in accordance with basic recipe (1) on page 13. Separate egg yolk and white while still warm and push yolk through sieve and mix with cooked rice. Mould rice on a large plate, arrange shrimps nicely, and top with sieved egg white. Arrange shallot greens around rice and place tomatoes around the edge of the plate.
Serves 6.

THE FLAVOR OF AUTUMN (Japan)

MUSHROOMS, chestnuts, ginko nuts, and other representative novelties of fall, cooked with shrimp and rice, is a Japanese favorite that every family would have at least once a year.

Ingredients
    3 cups rice, washed and drained
    2 oz. shrimp, peeled, head and black vein removed, washed, salted and peppered
    7 oz. chestnuts, peeled and cut in 1/2″ pieces
    3 ½ oz. mushrooms, cut in 1″ pieces
    1/3 cup ginko nuts, outside skin peeled, boiled and shelled
    3–3 ½ cups water
    1/3 cups mirin
    1 ½ tsps. salt

Utensils and Equipment
    Rice cooker
Method
    Place all of the ingredients in a rice cooker, level surface and turn on rice cooker. Let stand for 5 minutes after rice

cooker goes off, mix well and serve.
Serves 6.

WILD RICE RECIPES

A BOOK ON RICE cookery would be lacking if some mention were not made of wild rice—that gourmet's favorite. Although expensive because of the limited areas in which it grows and the need for hand harvesting, it is becoming increasingly popular. Wild rice is a tall, aquatic North American perennial grass, somewhat similar to shama millet. It grows in the Great Lakes region of North America, is harvested by Indians, for the most part, working from canoes in the shallow lake waters, and it is also known as Canada rice and Indian rice. Its flavor is distinctive and it has outstanding nutritive qualities. There are many ways to cook wild rice and these are usually explained on the box in which it is packed. However, the two most popular follow:

(1) *Boiling:* Wash rice carefully and thoroughly by placing in a sieve and pouring cold water over it until clean. For 1 cup rice, use $2\frac{1}{2}$ cups water and 1 tsp. salt. Put all ingredients in a heavy pot, bring to a boil, cover and simmer over low heat 40–50 minutes. Remove cover, stir with chopsticks or fork, and continue cooking 5 minutes more.

(2) *Steeping:* Put 1 cup wild rice in pot and add 4 cups boiling water. Let stand 20–25 minutes. Drain thoroughly. Repeat 3 times, adding 1 tsp. salt last time. Season and add butter to taste. Keep hot until served.

Creamed Wild Rice

Ingredients
  $1\frac{1}{2}$ cups wild rice (cooked by either method)
  1/2 cup heavy cream
  1/4 tsp. paprika
  Salt to suit taste
  2 tbsps. butter
  1 cup cream of mushroom soup (undiluted)

Utensils and Equipment
  Heavy skillets, saucepan
Method
  Combine cooked wild rice with scalded heavy cream, paprika and salt. Cook over low heat, stirring until cream absorbs.
  Melt butter in another skilled and pack rice mixture into it.
  Cook over low heat until well browned.
  Pour hot mushroom soup over and fold like an omelet.
  Serve hot.
  Serves 4.

Wild Rice, Mushrooms, and Almonds

Ingredients
  3 cups chicken stock
  2 small cans mushrooms (sliced)
  2 tbsps. finely chopped shallot
  1/2 cup blanched almonds, slivered

1/4 cup butter
1 cup wild rice (washed and drained)

Utensils and Equipment
Heavy skillet, baking dish
Method
Combine all ingredients except chicken stock in skillet and cook over medium heat about 20 minutes, stirring constantly. Heat oven to 325° and when almonds are browned, add chicken stock, stir and pour into baking dish. Cover tightly and bake about 1½ hours.
Serves 6–8.

Wild Rice Mould

Ingredients
1 cup wild rice (cooked by either method)
Clove of garlic (sliced) (optional)
1/4 cup butter
1/2 tsp. nutmeg
1/4 cup sherry

Utensils and Equipment
Bowl, ring mould (7″ size)
Method
Combine all ingredients and place in mould that has been well greased.
Place mould in pan of hot water and bake in moderate oven for 20 minutes. Run a knife around the edge of mould to loosen contents, invert on a platter. Fill center with your favorite creamed dish: chicken Stroganoff, chicken livers sauté, creamed spinach, etc.
Serves 4–6.

Wild Rice Stuffing for Fowl or Game

Ingredients
Chicken giblets (from 3½ lb. chicken)
4 cups water
1 tsp. salt
1 cup wild rice
1/4 cup butter
2 tbsps. chopped onion
1 tbsp. chopped green pepper
1/4 cup chopped celery

Utensils and Equipment
Saucepan, skillet
Method
Chop giblets and drop in boiling water to which salt has been added. Simmer 15 minutes. Remove giblets and stir wild rice into water. Cook until nearly done. Melt butter in skillet and sauté vegetables for 3 minutes. Drain rice and add it and giblets to sautéed vegetables. Suitable for 3½–4 lb. fowl or game.

Glossary

bay leaves: Leaves from a species of laurel tree; used in soups, with meats and fishes.

cardamon: It is used in confections, sauces, creams, sweet puddings, cakes, picklings, and in curry.

cinnamon: The bark stripped from young branches of the cinnamon tree; used in cookies, cakes, and with fruits.

clove: The unopened flower buds of the clove tree used to flavor soups, stocks, meats, and desserts.

coriander: The seed is ground and used in soups, meats; it is a constituent of curry powder.

cumin: The seed is ground and used in soups, meat dishes; it is a constituent of curry paste.

curry: Powders and paste are made up of various combinations of many spices, herbs, garlic and horseradish.

dill: It is commonly used in pickling as well as in meat and vegetable dishes, soups, salads, and sauces.

duke of argyll's tea tree: An Asiatic shrub, which is also called the matrimony vine.

glutinous rice: A type of rice which is stickier than the ordinary rice when cooked.

kelp: A brown seaweed; one type, called in Japanese *konbu*, is dried and used to make soup stock.

lemongrass: Cultivated in tropical regions, it has a lemonish odor: it is cooked with rice in Southeast Asian countries.

mirin: Sweet saké; used for cooking.

pepper: Black and white peppers are obtained from the same plant; black from the dried immature fruit and white pepper from the dried mature fruit with the hull removed. It is used as a condiment and seasoning in all "savory" dishes.

saffron: The dried stigma of a plant related to the crocus, it is used for the flavoring and coloring of cakes, soups, and rice.

saké: An alcoholic beverage made by the fermentation of rice; used commonly in cooking.

sesame: The seed has a nutty flavor and is used in bread, confections, and with rice; sesame oil also has a unique flavor and numerous used in Oriental cooking.

shirataki: Noodles made from devil's tongue starch; used in *sukiyaki* and other Japanese dishes (substitute: vermicelli).

shungiku: Vegetable of the chrysanthemum family; used in *sukiyaki* (substitute: watercress, spinach).

soy sauce: A brown liquid sauce made by subjecting boiled soy beans and roasted wheat flour to long fermentation, then to digestion in brine, and seasoned with salt.

tamarind: A tropical pod fruit containing sugar and various acids, such as citric and tartaric, in combination with potash.

tempura: Seafood and vegetables dipped in a special batter and deep fried in vegetable or sesame oil.

thyme: A pungently flavored herb used in stuffings, sauces, soups, and meat dishes.

tofu: Beancurd; roasted tofu is commonly used in *sukiyaki*.

tumeric: A dried rhizome or root from a plant in the ginger family. It is used extensively in curry powder and prepared mustard.